MW00682260

Titles in the series

www.amazingstoriesbooks.com

CRIME SCENE
INVESTIGATION

Solving crimes in the real world

by J. Fielding

PUBLISHED BY ALTITUDE PUBLISHING LTD.
1500 Railway Avenue, Canmore, Alberta T1W 1P6
www.amazingstoriesbooks.com
1-800-957-6888

Extreme care has been taken to ensure that the information contained
in this book is accurate and up to date at the time of printing. However,
neither the author nor the publisher is responsible for errors, omissions,
loss of income or anything else that may result from the information
contained in this book.

All web site URLs mentioned in this book were correct at the time of
printing. The publisher is not responsible for the content of external
web sites or changes which may have occurred since publication.

Publisher	Stephen Hutchings
Associate Publisher	Kara Turner
Canadian Editor	Brendan Wild
U.S. Editor	Julian S. Martin
Charts	Scott Dutton

We acknowledge the financial support of the Government
of Canada through the Book Publishing Industry Development
Program (BPIDP) for our publishing activities.

ALTITUDE GREENTREE PROGRAM
Altitude Publishing will plant twice as many trees as were used
in the manufacturing of this product.

Cataloging in Publication Data
Fielding, Jane
    CSI / J. Fielding.

(Late breaking amazing stories)
Includes bibliographical references.
ISBN 1-55265-304-8 (American mass market edition)
ISBN 1-55439-502-X (Canadian mass market edition)

   1. Crime scene searches. 2. Criminal investigation. 3. Evidence, Criminal.
I. Title. II. Series.

HV8073.F53 2006	363.25'2	C2005-907409-4	(Cdn.)
HV8073.F53 2006a	363.25'2	C2005-907422-1	(U.S.)

In Canada, Amazing Stories® is a registered trademark of Altitude Publishing
Canada Ltd. An application for the same trademark is pending in the U.S.

Printed and bound in Canada by Friesens
2 4 6 8 9 7 5 3

"Forensic Science is not used to predict the future but the past."

Henry C. Lee, criminalist

CONTENTS

John Allen Muhammad enters the courtroom
on August 5, 2003, during pre-trial motions in
Manassas, Virginia. For more on the story of
how Muhammad was tracked down, see chapter 1.

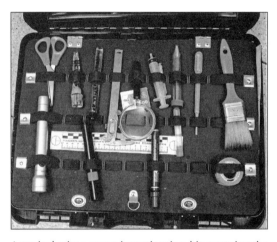

A typical crime scene investigation kit contains the tools used to find, collect, and record evidence at a crime scene. These tools include, among other things, a flashlight, marker pens, a ruler, calipers, evidence envelopes, fingerprint brushes, lifting tape, and dusting powders. For more behind-the-scenes information, see chapter 2.

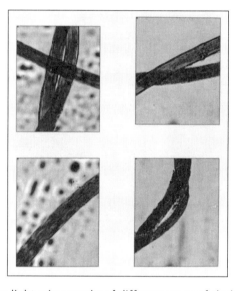

Four light micrographs of different types of clothing
fibers discovered at a crime scene. Analyzing fibers
under a microscope reveals identifying characteristics
such as textile weave, fiber count, and dye. For more
on the importance of trace evidence, see page 52.

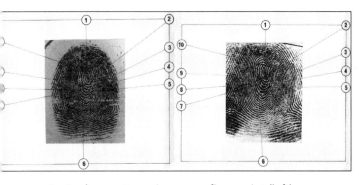

An "unknown," or crime scene fingerprint (left),
and matching "known" print (right). The points of
similarity used to make a positive identification are
marked on each by the fingerprint examiner.
For more on fingerprint analysis see page 55.

Richard Crafts is arrested on Jannuary 13,
1987, and charged with the murder of his wife.
For more on the story, see page 128.

Top: Footprints discovered
near the victim in "The Bloody
Footprint," page 151.

Right: The pattern of bloodstains at the crime scene can
impart vital information. For
more information, see page 70.

CHAPTER 1

Tracking Down a Serial Sniper

It seemed to come from out of nowhere. One minute, James Martin, a middle-aged program analyst, was strolling across the parking lot at the Shoppers Food Warehouse in Wheaton, Maryland. The next, his lifeless body was splayed out on the ground. A bullet from some unknown source had whizzed across the parking lot and lodged in Martin's chest, killing him instantly. The shooter had brazenly picked off his target so close to the Montgomery County

Police Station that several officers heard the shot and raced out to see what had happened. All they discovered, however, was the body of the program analyst in the half-empty parking lot. The shooter was nowhere in sight.

At 7:41 the next morning, James (Sonny) Buchanan was mowing the narrow strip of grass in front of the Colonial Dodge dealership on the Rockville Pike when he was gunned down.

Less than half an hour later, Pren Kumar Walekar nosed his taxicab up to the pumps at the Mobil station in Aspen Hill, three miles from the Dodge dealership. Before filling up, the cabbie ducked inside to pay for the gas and pick up a lottery ticket. He'd just returned to his cab and stuck the nozzle in the tank when he felt a searing pain in his chest. An MD at the next set of pumps looked up in time to see the cabbie clutch his chest and crumple to the ground. He rushed over and began administering first aid, but it was too late. The bullet, which shattered as it slammed into Walekar's chest, was fatal.

A sense of foreboding accompanied police as they raced from one crime scene to the next that sultry, Indian summer morning. Montgomery County, Maryland, wasn't the kind of community where drive-by shootings and gun battles in the streets were common events. The affluent Washington suburb had only 20 homicides in total the previous year. To have three killings in less than 24 hours was downright alarming.

But it wasn't just the number of killings that was disturbing. The three shootings bore similar hallmarks. Each victim appeared to have been shot by a high-powered rifle from a distance. There were no eyewitnesses, and, as far as police could discern, there was no connection between the victims. Furthermore, none of the shootings appeared to be drug related, nor did they resemble domestic disputes or crimes of passion. In fact, the inexplicably random nature of the killings and a near-complete lack of evidence left police baffled.

While Chief Charles Moose of the Montgomery County PD scrambled to deal with the first three homicides that October 3, 2002, he received a call informing him of a fourth. Sarah Ramos had been sitting on a bench outside the post office when a bullet struck her in the head. For Moose, the day was taking on a nightmarish aspect.

But it wasn't until the fifth fatal shooting—that of Lori Anne Lewis-Rivera—that the frightening reality of the situation took hold. The Montgomery County PD wasn't dealing with an ordinary, garden-variety killer. Rather, this killer was purposeful and unpredictable—a serial sniper.

After the Rivera killing, the first lead in the case finally surfaced. A witness claimed to have seen a white van speeding away from the Shell station where Lori Anne Rivera was shot while vacuuming out her minivan. It wasn't much, but after many tense hours with absolutely nothing to go on, it seemed like a godsend.

Another bonus was that for the first time

that day there was a pause in the killing spree. After dealing with four shootings in a single morning, the besieged Montgomery County PD was relieved by this respite. At the same time, police braced themselves for the next round.

The reprieve was short lived. At 9:15 that night, 72-year-old Pascal Charlot was slain while crossing the street on his nightly stroll. The sniper had claimed his sixth victim in a little over 24 hours.

At that point, the Department of Treasury's Bureau of Alcohol, Tobacco and Firearms (ATF), under the direction of Mike Bouchard, became involved in the investigation. Henceforth, all forensic evidence in the case would be handled by ATF's lab in Rockville, Maryland. This was welcome news to the Montgomery County investigators. ATF had the equipment and expertise to deal with an investigation of this magnitude. It also had tracking dogs trained to sniff out all manner of explosive materials, including gunpowder.

When taken to the scene of the Charlot

shooting, the dogs immediately zeroed in on the area from which the shot was fired. For the first time, investigators had an idea of the distance between the shooter and his target. It was a chilling revelation. There was no doubt that only an expert marksman using a high-powered rifle could make such a hit.

The next shooting occurred Friday, October 4, at 2:30 p.m. A 43-year-old woman was walking across the parking lot of a Michaels craft store in Fredericksburg, Virginia, just south of Montgomery County, when the sniper's bullet caught her in the upper back. Although critically wounded, the woman survived.

Once again, there were no witnesses, no clues. The fact that this shooting occurred in front of a Michaels craft store seemed significant, however. Less than an hour before James Martin was shot, a bullet had shattered the window of the Michaels store on Aspen Hill Rd. Was it simply a coincidence? investigators wondered. Or was the craft store chain their link between the sniper and his victims?

By Friday, Walter Dandridge, Jr., ATF's principal firearms analyst on the case, concluded that the same gun had been used in all of the shootings, including the latest in Fredericksburg. He had also determined that the caliber of ammunition was either .223 or .221. With this information, investigators made an educated guess about the make and model of rifle the sniper was using.

Before long, everyone in the immediate area known to possess a weapon that fired .223 or .221 caliber ammunition was subjected to the task force's intense scrutiny. Dozens of suspicious individuals, gun fanatics, survivalists, and extremists were put under surveillance. And one by one, each was eventually cleared.

While investigators struggled to establish solid leads, the sniper took the weekend off. The pause in the killing did little to ease the tension and anxiety that gripped Montgomery County. This anxiety would develop into full-blown panic with the next shooting.

On Monday morning at 8:09, Iran Brown climbed out of his aunt's car in front of Benjamin Tasker Middle School. As he turned to wave goodbye, a bullet pierced the 13-year-old's chest. He was whisked to a nearby clinic and then airlifted to the Children's National Medical Center in Washington. The bullet was lodged dangerously close to his heart, and he had sustained serious damage to several organs. Miraculously, the critically wounded boy survived.

Already suffering shellshock, this latest shooting plunged the community into hysteria. Outraged by this latest act, Chief Charles Moose was unable to control his emotions during his next press conference. "All our victims have been innocent and defenseless," he tearfully exclaimed, "but now we're stepping over the line. Shooting a kid—it's getting to be really, really personal now." At that point, Moose made the decision to request the FBI's assistance with the case.

Local investigators were already busy

searching the latest crime scene. As they beat the bushes where the sniper had lain in wait, they discovered a vital piece of evidence. Half hidden in the underbrush across the street from the Benjamin Tasker Middle School, they found a single tarot card.

The death card featured an image of a skeleton dressed in armor atop the back of a white horse. Traditionally, the death card symbolizes transformation and rebirth. It also alludes to the fact that death doesn't discern between young or old, rich or poor. The sniper's message was clear: no one is safe. Priests, politicians, bureaucrats, welfare recipients, grandparents, parents, and children—all were potential targets.

Written in a shaky hand across the top of the card was a declaration: "Dear Policeman, I am God." This was followed by the warning, "Do not release to media."

The tarot card was immediately dispatched to the forensic lab. There, it was examined for fingerprints and swabbed for DNA. Neither was discovered. Before the card was released to task force members, the sniper's handwriting and the ink used to pen the message were analyzed. Disappointingly, no useful information was gained.

Despite the fact the tarot card yielded no trace evidence, its discovery put the investigation on a new footing. It was a relief to possess something tangible to focus on, beyond bullet fragments. In addition, investigators viewed the killer's decision to leave the card at the scene as a positive sign. The fact the sniper left a message for them, however brief, set the stage for communication between the sniper and police.

The killing didn't stop, however.

Two days later, on October 9, at 8:15 p.m., Dean Harold Meyers, a 53-year-old civil engineer who had survived the Vietnam War and was decorated with the Purple Heart, became the sniper's ninth victim. Meyers was gunned down while filling up at a Sunoco station near Manassas, Virginia.

By now, the investigation into what was

dubbed the tarot card sniper case had ballooned into a massive operation. An army of police, investigators, crime lab technicians, detectives, and others were working feverishly around the clock to isolate a suspect. The task force included nine police departments and several federal agencies, including the FBI, the U.S. Marshall's Service, the U.S. Secret Service, the Department of Defense, and ATF, among others. Dozens of suspects were investigated daily, and hundreds of leads were followed.

In addition to the feds, the media circus had also arrived in town. The attention of the nation was riveted on Montgomery County and the drama playing out there. For many residents of the staid Washington suburb, a serial sniper stalking their community was as traumatic as the terrorist attacks of the previous fall. The sight of officers in flak jackets swarming the streets escalated the tension and fear that cloaked the city. It seemed normal life had been suspended indefinitely. Few dared venture out unless absolutely necessary. Children no longer walked to school. Stores were empty. Outdoor sporting events and field trips were cancelled. Everyone huddled indoors—watching CNN and waiting for the next development in the case.

After the Meyers shooting, two days passed without incident. Then, at 9:30 a.m. on October 11, the sniper struck again. Again he targeted someone at a gas station. Kenneth Bridges, a 53-year-old father of six from Philadelphia, was filling up at an Exxon station off I-95 when he was cut down not 50 yards from a state trooper.

Three days later, on Columbus Day, 47-year-old Linda Franklin was loading purchases from the Home Depot in Falls Church, VA, into the back of her car when she was shot in the head. Franklin, an FBI analyst and mother of two young children, died instantly.

It was eerily quiet for a full five days after the Franklin killing. Then, as some began to wonder whether it was safe to breathe a sigh of relief, another shooting occurred. On Saturday, October

19, a 37-year-old male was shot while walking across the parking lot of the Ponderosa Steak House in Ashland, Virginia. Though seriously wounded, the victim survived the shooting. He was rushed to hospital and operated on immediately. Surgeons removed part of his stomach, as well as his pancreas and spleen. It wasn't until the victim was out of danger, however, that they managed to successfully retrieve the bullet during a second operation. As investigators predicted, the bullet matched all the others.

Immediately after the Ponderosa shooting, the crime scene was secured and a painstaking search for evidence commenced. The scene was a large parking lot surrounded by dense woods. The fact that it was pitch black and pouring rain by the time the search began made the task extremely difficult. Again, tracking dogs were brought to the scene to sniff out explosive materials. The canines led investigators directly to the spot where the shot was fired. There, they discovered a spent shell casing.

The search continued throughout the night and into the next day. Sixteen hours of shoulder-to-shoulder fingertip searching yielded little more than the shell casing. Investigators were soaked through, exhausted, and demoralized when they finally discovered the sniper's note. The hand-written, four-page note had been sealed carefully inside two plastic bags and tacked to a tree.

The note was rushed directly to a lab where it was processed for fingerprints and DNA before task force members were granted access. Again, however, hopes of collecting a fingerprint or DNA from the evidence were soon quashed. Neither the baggies that held the note nor the paper it was written on yielded anything in the way of trace evidence. The note's contents, however, offered much more.

The oddly phrased letter demanded $10 million in exchange for ending the killings. The money was to be deposited in a Bank of America Platinum Visa account. The amount demanded was staggering. Worse, however, was the chilling threat that accompanied it: "Your children are not safe anywhere at anytime."

The implication was clear: if the sniper's demands weren't met, more children would be targeted. With the body count already at 10, the task force wasn't prepared to take chances. Wheels were set in motion to secure the money and arrange the drop.

For some time, investigators had suspected that more than one person was involved in the shootings. There had to be both a shooter and a driver, they reasoned. It was the only way the sniper could flee the scene so quickly after each shooting. The fact that the author of the second note used the plurals "us" and "we" throughout appeared to confirm these suspicions. If two people were involved, it seemed likely at least one had been in the military at some point. Throughout military sniper training, trainees work in pairs: one performs the role of spotter, the other is the shooter. It was beginning to look more and more as though the suspect might be an ex-GI.

Another significant clue from the note was the sniper's claim to have tried repeatedly to contact authorities through the task force hotline. He was outraged that his calls weren't patched directly through to Chief Moose. Because of this failure to connect, he asserted, five additional lives had been lost. He also ranted about having tried to contact the police through "a priest in Ashland." Although these ravings were vague and sounded mad, the task force took every word seriously. Investigators immediately followed up on this lead and tracked down the "priest."

Monsignor William Sullivan was the pastor of St. Anne's Church in Ashland. When located and questioned about the sniper's phone call, the monsignor recalled vividly the conversation with the person who introduced himself as "God." The caller, he remembered, demanded that the monsignor convey a message to police for him. He also recalled that Montgomery, Alabama, surfaced several times during the course of the rambling conversation'.

While the task force investigated this new lead, the 13th shooting occurred. At 5:56 Tuesday morning, 35-year-old bus driver Conrad Johnson was preparing to set out on his route when a bullet struck him in the abdomen. Johnson was rushed to the hospital but died on the operating table.

The shot had come from a wooded area next to the bus depot in Aspen Hill. Again, investigators cordoned off the crime scene and began to hunt for clues. During the search, another note was discovered. Again the sniper threatened the safety of the children of Montgomery County. And again the level of anxiety in the community soared.

In the meantime, authorities' investigation of the sniper's earlier remarks about events in Montgomery, Alabama, generated a pivotal breakthrough. Upon contacting the Montgomery

PD, investigators discovered there had, indeed, been a recent, unsolved homicide that fit the sniper's modus operandi to a T.

The homicide had occurred two weeks before the killing spree in Maryland began. On September 21, two women had been shot—one fatally—outside a liquor store in Montgomery. Investigators in Alabama reported they hadn't recovered much in the way of evidence—a few bullet fragments from the body of the victim and a magazine about firearms dropped by the suspect as he fled the scene. Montgomery police didn't know that evidence they had in their possession contained the clue necessary to crack the case that had rocked Montgomery County and gripped the nation for more than two weeks.

The task force immediately had the magazine processed for trace evidence. After all previous failures to find solid evidence, they had low expectations. But when the magazine was fumed, a latent fingerprint materialized in a corner of one of the glossy pages. Although it was helpful to obtain a fingerprint, authorities still had to locate a match or the print was useless. The print was run through IAFIS, the FBI's fingerprint identification database. Amazingly, they got a hit.

The print belonged to 17-year-old Lee Boyd Malvo, a Jamaican citizen whose fingerprints were on file with Immigration and Naturalization Services. (The task force later discovered Malvo had been stopped by a Montgomery County police officer on October 2. A check run on the youth indicated no outstanding warrants and he was released.) A background check on Malvo revealed that his mother had a boyfriend who was like a father to the youth.

Forty-one-year-old John Allen Williams (a.k.a. John Allen Muhammad) was a Gulf War veteran. He was also an expert marksman. The native of Baton Rouge, Louisiana, was wanted on an outstanding firearms charge as well as a shoplifting charge. He was a fractious character who had battled with both his ex-wives as well as his superiors in the military. A father of four, Muhammad had waged intense legal battles with his ex-wives for custody of his children. He'd also threatened to kill one of his ex-wives. As a result, a restraining order had been issued against him. The ex, it turned out, was an employee of a Michaels craft store.

It seemed almost too good to be true. After dozens of blunders, false leads, and dead ends, the task force finally had a solid suspect in the case. Now they had to find him. A check with DMV turned up a John Allen Muhammad of Tacoma, Washington. Apparently, Muhammad didn't own a white van, but he did have a blue, 1990 Chevy Caprice registered in his name.

A team of investigators rushed to Tacoma and descended on Muhammad's last known address—a blue duplex in a lower-middle class neighborhood. The duplex was turned inside out and neighbors interrogated. When several disgruntled neighbors mentioned Muhammad's irritating habit of firing off round after round of ammunition at the tree stump in his backyard at night, the stump was promptly excavated and shipped to the Maryland lab for processing.

In the meantime, task force members requested warrants for the arrest of Lee Boyd Malvo and John Allen Muhammad. With warrants issued, they held a press briefing and identified the two as suspects in the case. Not wanting to alarm or forewarn the suspects into bolting, authorities didn't mention the make or model of their vehicle. The media, however, managed to ferret out this information. CNN broke the news shortly afterward and reported that police were seeking suspects John Allen Muhammad and Lee Boyd Malvo, who were driving a 1990 Caprice with New Jersey plates. Not long thereafter, someone spotted the Chevy Caprice parked at a rest stop at Exit 42 off I-70, and called 911.

Just after midnight on October 24, police barricaded all on- and off-ramps for miles on either side of Exit 42. Tactical units moved in and SWAT teams surrounded the rest stop. More than 100 heavily armed officers closed in on the Caprice; many more formed an outer perimeter in the woods behind the rest stop.

At precisely 3:19 a.m., John Allen Muhammad and Lee Boyd Malvo were wrenched from sleep when the Caprice's windows were smashed with sledgehammers and flash-bang grenades were lobbed inside. Surrounding the car, dozens of keyed up officers in helmets and flak jackets trained high-powered weapons on the pair. While helicopters circled overhead, flooding the scene with blinding light and throbbing sound, the leader of the SWAT team commanded the suspects to step out of the car with their hands in the air. Finding themselves with little choice, the culprits meekly complied. Within seconds, the pair that had terrorized Maryland and Virginia for three weeks were spread eagle on the pavement.

Once Malvo and Muhammad were hauled away, a team of investigators secured the perimeter of the scene. When ATF's mobile crime lab arrived, an intense search for evidence ensued. Because there were no eyewitnesses to any of the shootings, the prosecution's entire case depended on circumstantial evidence. There could be no screw-ups. Every shred of physical evidence available had to be collected and documented with the utmost care. To ensure no evidence found in the "sniper's nest" could possibly be contested in court, the Caprice wasn't touched until investigators had a search warrant in hand. The car was then cautiously loaded on a truck and transported to the Maryland lab for processing.

At the lab, every inch of the Caprice was scrutinized. It was photographed inside and out, fumed for fingerprints, and swabbed for DNA. The car, which had been bought at Sure Shot Auto Sales in New Jersey, proved one of the best pieces of probative evidence recovered in the investigation.

The "sniper's nest" was an apt moniker for

the vehicle, which had been converted into a practical staging area for the killers. Two holes—one above the other—had been drilled in the trunk. These were just the right size to accommodate the rifle muzzle and scope. The suspects had placed a platform in the trunk to stand the tripod on. This supported the rifle barrel and scope at just the right height to match the holes. Socks the same shade as the car were stuffed into the holes to camouflage them when empty. As well, part of the backseat had been removed to enable the shooter to stretch out comfortably while taking aim. Each of these modifications was thoroughly photographed and documented as evidence.

Inside, the Caprice had a disheveled, lived-in look. Empty bottles, fast-food containers, dirty clothes, and papers were strewn across the floors and seats. The investigators sifted though the junk, documenting and bagging each item.

Among the empty coffee cups and dirty laundry, they discovered a stolen laptop computer and GPS. It now became clear how the killers had always managed their slick getaways: the computer contained files of detailed maps of the area. Each of the shooting sites was marked with a skull icon.

Muhammad's military training and penchant for chess were evident in the tactical strategy he'd used to target the best killing locations and to map out all possible escape routes well ahead of time. The snipers also had a set of walkie-talkies in the car. With these, the spotter in the driver's seat could easily inform the shooter when the coast was clear, or if there was any sign of trouble. The customization of the car, along with the presence of the computer, GPS, and walkie-talkies, provided indisputable proof of the pair's murderous intentions.

It wasn't until the investigators removed the remainder of the backseat, however, that they hit the evidentiary jackpot. Tucked away under the seat was the Bushmaster XM-15 E2S, a high-powered assault rifle that fired .223

caliber ammunition.

They had their smoking gun.

The Bushmaster was first taken to the FBI lab and analyzed for trace evidence before it was turned over to ATF for firearms analysis. Under the lead of Walter Dandridge, seven ATF examiners conducted the firearms tests. In order to determine if a bullet has been fired from a suspect weapon, analysts begin by firing a test round from the recovered firearm. They then compare the test bullet with those recovered from the crime scene, using a comparison microscope. This high-powered microscope allows the examiner to view the two bullets side by side. If the striations are identical on both, it's a positive match.

Dandridge and his team compared each bullet fragment collected over the course of the investigation with the test bullets fired from the Bushmaster. Every striation, breech mark, and firing pin impression was analyzed and re-analyzed. Once all seven examiners had completed their tests, ATF was able to declare, without any doubt, that this was the weapon used to kill all 12 victims (including the woman in Alabama) and to wound three others. This analysis, along with the laptop and GPS, the walkie-talkies, the silencer and scopes, the fingerprint, bullet fragments, the sniper's notes, and the modifications to the Caprice added up to a monumental pile of evidence.

Weeks of painstaking labor by the crime scene investigators paid off in the end. On November 17, 2003, John Allen Muhammad was convicted of capital murder. He was later sentenced to death by Virginia judge LeRoy Millette, Jr. His juvenile partner, Lee Boyd Malvo, was sentenced to life in prison without the possibility of parole.

CHAPTER 2

Behind the Scenes

CSI Fact and Fiction

In these times of reality TV and gritty, "realistic" crime dramas, more than a few of us, it seems, are having difficulty discerning between fact and fiction. For example, the fictional TV show *CSI: Crime Scene Investigation* has had a dramatic impact on real-life forensic investigations over the past few years. Experts say the rise in popularity of shows such as *CSI* has distorted the public's perception of forensic science and has produced what is now known as the "CSI effect." This effect has impacted everything from enrollments in university forensics programs to the types of evidence presented in court.

CSI's glitzy spin on the science of fighting crime has attracted hordes of wannabes to the field and caused applications for and enrollments in university forensic science programs to skyrocket. By the same token, it has also granted lab geeks a newfound popularity on campus. These days, knowing the difference between gas chromatography and mass spectrometry doesn't automatically impose pariah status. In fact, in some circles it might be considered a turn on.

Another consequence of *CSI*'s popularity, however, is that it has generated some wildly unrealistic expectations about the timelines and technology used for crime fighting. Today, many victims of crime are reportedly dismayed by the length of time required to solve crimes,

CSI ON TV

CSI creator Anthony Zuiker first pitched the idea for the crime drama to ABC in 1999; they turned it down, however, and declared it was too technical for the average viewer to comprehend. The show first aired on CBS in the fall of 2000 and immediately shot to the top of the ratings charts. Since then, two spin offs—*CSI: Miami* and *CSI: New York*—have been introduced. In June of 2005, *CSI* came in second in the Neilson ratings with an estimated audience of 15 million viewers.

the technologies available to investigators, and the capabilities of crime labs in general.

The CSI effect has also influenced what goes on in courtrooms. In recent years there's been a marked change in the attitude of jurors concerning the evidence presented during criminal trials. These days, juries expect scientific evidence to be presented. If no such evidence exists, or is irrelevant to the case, they want to know why. Exasperated judges have been overheard instructing juries to forget what they've seen on television and reminding them, "This is not *CSI;* it's real life."

In fact, real crime scene investigations bear

only a passing resemblance to those portrayed on prime-time TV. Fictional crime scene investigators have more state-of-the-art, high-tech equipment and nifty gadgets at their disposal than James Bond, the FBI, *and* the CIA combined. They also strut around on the job decked out in fashionable street garb. Oh, and notice that they *always* stumble upon intriguing evidence, which inevitably comes in handy for teasing confessions out of suspects during interrogations. What's more, they manage to put all the pieces together and nail their suspect within, thank heaven, 60 minutes.

Meanwhile, many of their real-life counterparts make do with cobbled together crime kits and aging lab equipment. It takes them weeks or months or, sometimes, even years to solve crimes. Worse still—rather than tank tops and jeans, they're made to wear extremely unstylish officer protection suits—fondly known as "bunny suits"—on the scene.

But fashionable apparel and high-tech

gadgets aren't the only differences between fact and fiction in the CSI world. In the real world, many forensic investigators rarely visit the scene of the crime. And they *never* interview witnesses or suspects. In fact, in reality, the only place most investigators come face to face with suspects and witnesses is in court.

Within most law enforcement agencies, interrogating suspects and witnesses, and following up leads, is the responsibility of the detectives of the major crimes unit. While detectives conduct surveillance, and search out and round up suspects, the forensic

CRIME LABS

Chicago's brutal St. Valentine's Day Massacre in 1929 led to the development of America's first crime lab, under the direction of Calvin Goddard. Prior to this event, crime-scene evidence was sent to hospitals and universities for processing. Today, numerous groups and organizations are involved in the business of crime scene investigation in North America. Dozens of private labs provide forensic services. In addition, most law enforcement agencies have forensic identification units and crime labs within their organizations.

people are busy in the lab analyzing evidence.

The Scene of the Crime

Crimes occur in every kind of environment imaginable, from school playgrounds to seedy motel rooms. A crime scene can cover several acres, or it can be confined to a space as small as the interior of a vehicle. And although crimes themselves may be similar in nature, each scene is unique.

Like fragile ecosystems, crime scenes must be handled with care. One blunder can destroy precious evidence and compromise an entire case. Therefore, qualified forensic investigators don't simply charge into an area where a crime has been committed and begin poking around at random the way their TV counterparts do. Because each crime scene is unique, the approach to each scene is tailored to suit the circumstances. Nevertheless, there are certain procedures and protocols that investigators follow in each instance.

The first and most essential step in every

investigation is to secure the scene and establish a perimeter. The police barrier serves to protect the integrity of the crime scene. Having reporters and curious onlookers tramping around would only disturb and contaminate the scene and could destroy precious evidence. Once the perimeter is established, investigators don coveralls (the bunny suit), latex gloves, and, on occasion, surgical masks before entering the site. This garb is worn in order to prevent cross contamination of the scene: investigators shedding their own hairs and fibers would only make matters more complex.

An initial walk-through, or preliminary survey, of the scene usually precedes a more thorough search that follows. At this stage the obvious evidence is marked. The scene, and each piece of evidence, is documented with photographs, videos, sketches, and a written narrative. The narrative includes descriptions of everything in and around the scene including, among other things, the weather and lighting conditions. After investigators complete the initial walk-through, the more intensive "fingertip search" commences.

Fragile evidence can easily be obliterated by wind, rain, or snow. And because some of the most valuable evidence—such as fingerprints, footprints, tire tracks, and tool marks—is often discovered at points of entry and exit, these perimeter areas are the first to be searched.

Exhibit A

Crime scene investigation is all about the evidence. The purpose and focus of CSI is to discover, collect, identify, and analyze evidence that will help solve a crime. An investigator's skill lies in determining what *is* evidence and what is not.

Evidence can be anything tangible that links a suspect to a crime. Forensic investigators are always conscious that anything at a given scene may be evidence—no matter how banal it may seem. It can be a half-melted candle or a pile of woodchips. It can be tool marks, bullet holes, cigarette butts, insects, hair, fibers, pollen, dust, glass, bone fragments, or stone chips. It can be bite marks, ligature marks, cuts, slashes, stab wounds, or bruising. It can be saliva, semen, urine, or blood. It can also be a sample of handwriting, records of phone calls, emails, or other documents. Anything that can be collected, documented, and analyzed becomes forensic evidence in a criminal investigation.

Tainted Evidence

How evidence is handled after it's been discovered is critical to an investigation. Once collected, each item must be properly documented, labeled, packaged, and transported to the lab where it will be analyzed. In order for the court to be certain of the authenticity of a piece of evidence, investigators are required to maintain a history, or "chain of custody," for each item. The chain of custody is a record of the name of each person who handles the evidence, along with the date and time at which it was in that individual's possession. Maintaining the continuity and integrity of the chain of custody is imperative. Each item must be accounted for from the moment it is seized until it is presented at the trial.

As the outcome of the O. J. Simpson case demonstrated, investigators who fail to collect and document the evidence properly can jeopardize an entire case. At the beginning of the Simpson trial, the prosecution declared they had a "mountain of evidence" to prove the celebrity's guilt. There was, among other items, the bloody glove, the stocking cap, and the blood found throughout Simpson's house and in his Bronco. Due to the LAPD's sloppy search tactics and the glaring gaps in the chain of custody, however, the evidence was, in the words of the defense, "contaminated, compromised, and corrupted." Most of the evidence presented was deemed inadmissible, and the remainder was viewed with suspicion by the jury, who acquitted the defendant.

Trace Evidence

Whenever we enter a room we change it in some way. We leave fingerprints on each surface we touch, we shed hairs and fibers, and we deposit and pick up debris on the soles of our shoes. As the great, 20th-century criminalist Edmond Locard said, "Every contact leaves a trace."

Therefore, no matter how carefully a criminal tries to cover his tracks, he always leaves behind telltale traces of his presence. Furthermore, he inevitably takes evidence from the scene away with him. These traces may be as minute as a single hair from the suspect's or the victim's head or body, or as non-descript as particles of soil or sand tracked in on his shoes. To investigators, the smallest fragments of debris found on the suspect or at the crime scene are viewed as potential clues.

Trace evidence is often transferred through physical contact. If an intruder smashes a window during a break in, for example, microscopic glass fragments are likely to cling to his clothing and shoes. If he enters the scene by squeezing through the broken window, fibers from his clothing may be found around the point of entry. If a victim struggles with his or her attacker, hair and fibers will likely be exchanged.

Trace evidence is everywhere in our environment. And whether man-made or natural, it's almost always produced in large quantities. The hairs shed by humans and animals; the fibers from our clothing, carpets, or upholstery; the soil from our gardens; the pollen, seeds, and debris from plants and trees that surround our

THE FIRST INVESTIGATORS

The story of crime scene investigation in the west began with Sir Arthur Conan Doyle, the creator of Sherlock Holmes, in the late 1800s. Doyle was a medical doctor and a pioneer in the field of forensic investigation. His writing had a major influence on a French medical–legal student by the name of Edmond Locard. After graduating, Locard went on to become one of the world's first forensic scientists. His success in solving crimes by using scientific analysis led to his nickname, the "Sherlock Holmes of France." Locard's principle, "every contact leaves a trace," is the basic premise that underlies all modern crime scene investigative techniques.

homes and worksites; the glass fragments from broken windows, headlights, or glassware; and the paint chips from our vehicles are all trace evidence.

The abundant nature of trace evidence makes it both a blessing and a curse for investigators. Because it's produced in abundance, it usually lacks much in the way of distinguishing characteristics. Therefore, searching for matching fibers or glass fragments is similar to looking for one particular grain of sand in a desert.

But occasionally investigators get a break. For instance, when the body of 32-year-old Shirley Duguay was discovered in a shallow grave on Prince Edward Island in May 1995, investigators also found a man's bloodstained jacket in a plastic bag nearby. A few fine, white hairs were found on the jacket. Douglas Beamish, Duguay's former common law husband, was the prime suspect in the case. When the Royal Canadian Mounted Police (RCMP) called on Beamish, they noted he had a white cat, named Snowball. A sample of Snowball's blood was collected and sent for DNA testing along with the hairs found on the jacket. Sure enough, Snowball's DNA matched that of the hairs from the jacket. As a result, Douglas Beamish was arrested, tried, and convicted of the murder of Shirley Duguay.

Fingerprints

On the night of September 19, 1910, Clarence B. Hiller was shot and killed by an intruder in his suburban Chicago home. Shortly after the shooting occurred, two beat cops stopped a suspicious looking character by the name of Thomas Jennings in the neighborhood of the Hiller home. Jennings was disheveled and his clothes were blood stained. When the officers searched him and discovered a loaded revolver in his pocket, they immediately placed Jennings under arrest. A background check revealed that Jennings had just finished serving a sentence for burglary.

Meanwhile, sleuths were busy combing

the Hiller home for clues to the identity of the owner's killer. Coincidentally, a few hours before he was killed, Clarence Hiller had painted a porch railing outside the kitchen window. When the investigators examined the rail, they discovered quite compelling evidence: imprinted in the fresh paint was a perfect set of four fingerprints.

THE MARK OF A CRIMINAL

Henry Faulds, a Scottish physician working at the Tsukiji Hospital in Tokyo, was the first to realize that the distinctiveness of fingerprints make them ideal for identifying criminal suspects. Faulds' discovery progressed a step further when Juan Vucetich, an Argentinean police official, developed the first criminal fingerprint identification system in 1891.

In 1910, in North America, the practice of identifying a suspect by matching fingerprints found at a crime scene with those of known criminals was in its infancy. Scotland Yard had been using this revolutionary practice for almost a decade by that time, but it was slower to catch on in the United States and Canada. Fortunately, the Chicago

PD was one of the first in the country to adopt the system.

Because of his previous conviction, Thomas Jennings's prints were on file. When experts compared the felon's prints with those found at the crime scene, they were declared a positive match. Consequently, Jennings was charged with the murder of Clarence Hiller.

But the prosecution's case was not conclusive. They had no eyewitnesses and very little circumstantial evidence other than the fingerprints discovered at the scene. To make matters worse, fingerprints had never before been introduced as evidence in a criminal trial in the United States. In fact, the prosecution was unsure whether the court would even allow them to be presented. If permitted to do so, prosecutors could only guess how the jury would react to this newfangled scientific evidence.

Leaving nothing to chance, the prosecution lined up not one, but four, fingerprint experts to testify at trial. Three had been trained at Scotland Yard. The fourth, Inspector Edward Foster of the RCMP, was the man responsible for establishing Canada's National Fingerprint Bureau. After hearing the testimony of these specialists, the jury was convinced of Jennings's guilt. On February 1, 1911, Thomas Jennings became the first person in the U.S. to be convicted and sentenced to death, based on fingerprint evidence.

Jennings appealed the decision to the Supreme Court of Illinois. His lawyer argued against the admissibility of fingerprint evidence. But the court ruled against him, maintaining that fingerprinting was, indeed, an acceptable scientific means of identifying criminals.

For nearly a century after the Jennings trial, fingerprints were considered solid scientific evidence. And despite recent controversy concerning the soundness of the science behind the practice of friction ridge identification, fingerprints are still deemed to be among the most significant evidence collected at any crime scene.

Loops, Whorls, and Arches

The belief that no two people share the same fingerprints, and that this uniqueness makes fingerprints the only "infallible" means of identification, has prevailed since the beginning of 20th century. Friction ridges, which form on our fingertips before birth, are what make each individual's fingerprints distinct from those of every other person on earth.

Friction ridges remain virtually unchanged from cradle to grave. Because they form within the dermis rather than at the epidermis (the outer layer of skin, which peels when sun burnt), they can't be eliminated permanently. Even if the epidermis is sanded off or surgically removed, friction ridges grow back in patterns identical to the originals—a fact more than one culprit has discovered the hard way. Once fingerprinting became an accepted means to identify and thereby convict felons in the 1930s, many gangsters reportedly went to great lengths to have their prints altered or removed, only to have the originals grow back a few months later.

Friction ridges fall into three basic patterns, known as loops, whorls, and arches. Everyone has a unique combination of these patterns on each finger (and toe). Within these three categories are subcategories, such as tented arches and radial loops. In addition, a variety of other minute details, known as minutia, exist among the loops, whorls, and arches, and thus individualize these patterns further.

Whorls are the most common of the three basic friction ridge patterns. Approximately one third of the population's fingerprints conform to this pattern. The least common pattern is arch fingerprints.

Visible, Plastic, and Latent

At a crime scene, investigators look for three types of fingerprints—visible, plastic, and latent. *Visible prints* are those left on surfaces by someone with blood, grease, paint, or a similar substance on their fingers. *Plastic prints* are also

FINGERPRINT DETAILS

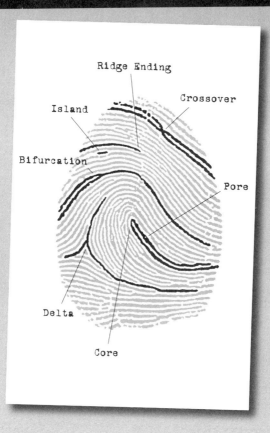

visible; they are a three-dimensional type found in materials such as putty or unfired clay. *Latent prints,* however, aren't visible to the naked eye.

When discovered, visible prints are photographed. Then investigators often seize the object they're found on and take it to the lab for processing rather than attempt to lift such prints at the scene.

Latent prints are more difficult to find than visible prints. Experienced sleuths, however, know where to look for them. Dusting for latent prints usually begins around the entrance and exit points of a crime scene because prints are most likely to be found in these areas.

The traditional method of revealing latent prints is to dust surfaces with carbon powder. Carbon dusting is quick, easy, and inexpensive. It's also messy. Dusting involves coating a surface with finely ground carbon or aluminum powder using a soft brush. Because our fingertips secrete sweat, which is frequently mixed with sebaceous oils from the face, a residue in the pattern of our friction ridges remains on surfaces we touch. The colored dust clings to the oily residue and renders the latent print visible.

Once exposed, the fingerprint is photographed. A low-tack adhesive tape mounted on acetate is then used to lift the print from the surface. Afterward, the lifted fingerprint is placed on a file card that contains pertinent information about the case.

In addition to carbon dusting, investigators now have a few high-tech means at their disposal to reveal latent prints. These include UV, laser, and alternative light source (ALS) lights. These lights, whether used alone or with fluorescent powders, cause latent prints to glow, or fluoresce, in the dark.

In order to reveal latent prints on porous surfaces—such as cloth and paper—investigators use a process known as fuming. This involves exposing the paper or cloth that holds the print to the vapors of a chemical such as iodine, silver nitrate, or ninhydrin in a fuming chamber. Once these toxic vapors are absorbed into the oily residue of the fingerprint, the prints become visible.

A revolutionary development in finger-printing in recent years has been the discovery of super glue as a chemical enhancer of latent prints. The vapors of the active ingredient in super glue—cynoacrylate—are extremely effective for exposing prints on plastic surfaces. Prior to this discovery, revealing latent prints on plastic surfaces was all but impossible.

Matching Prints:
Known and Unknown

Finding and lifting fingerprints is only half the battle for criminalists. Crime-scene prints are useless without also having the suspect's prints for comparison. In the first half of the 20th century, fingerprint matching was a tedious and time-consuming process.

The first scheme for matching prints was developed in 1896 by Sir Edward Richard Henry, of England. This standardized 10-print system classified fingerprints according to the different patterns of friction ridge formations on all 10 fingers, assigning a numerical value to each one. The Henry system resulted in an unwieldy database of over 1,000 different codes, with each set of new prints filed under a specific code. At the time, the Henry system seemed revolutionary because fingerprint examiners only had to search through *known* prints that bore the same code as the crime-scene prints, rather than search through *every* set of prints on file.

The trouble with the Henry system was that it required a complete set of 10 prints in order to work adequately. As all crime scene investigators know, the odds of finding a full set of prints at a crime scene are abysmal. In fact, finding one or two full, clear prints is a rarity. If the perpetrator doesn't wear gloves and fingerprints *are* found at the scene, they're usually partial or smudged, or the details are obscured by markings or debris from the surface on which they are discovered. Therefore, the Henry system was hardly practical.

Today, crime-scene prints are run through databases such as the FBI's Integrated Automated Fingerprint Identification System (IAFIS). In seconds, the computer generates a list of possible matches. The fingerprint examiner then compares the crime-scene print with the known prints and looks for matching details. (The number of matching details required to declare a positive identification varies from country to country.) Once the examiner feels he or she has a match, the print is then re-examined by a second fingerprint examiner for verification before a positive match is declared.

Shoeprints and Tire Tracks

Although not quite as probative as fingerprints, shoeprints and tire tracks often provide investigators with significant clues to crimes. Because footwear impressions are highly individual, they can be quite useful for linking a suspect to a crime scene. By analyzing these prints, investigators can ascertain details, such as how many suspects were at the scene, their sex, approximate height and weight, and gait.

The two types of footprints investigators look for at a crime scene are three-dimensional impressions and two-dimensional tracks. *Two-dimensional* footprints are those created when someone walks across a hard surface with mud, blood, paint, or a similar substance on the soles of his or her shoes. *Three-dimensional* impressions are those left in soft ground, mud, or dirt. When discovered at the scene, both types of footprints are thoroughly photographed next to a measuring scale. If possible, two-dimensional prints are lifted in a manner akin to that used for fingerprints. Casts are made of three-dimensional prints with plaster of paris or dental stone. Impressions in snow are pretreated with a wax spray that stabilizes the prints before plaster is poured into them. Tire tracks are treated in the same manner as footprints. When discovered, they are photographed and, if possible, casts are made of the impressions.

Characteristics

There are two types of characteristics associated with footprints: individual characteristics and class characteristics. *Individual characteristics* are the scars, pits, scrapes, and stones acquired by footwear through everyday wear and tear. *Class characteristics* are those created by a manufacturer. These include the dizzying array of patterns impressed on shoe soles. All sorts of patterns—from zigzags, diamonds, bars, circles, and waves, to manufacturers' logos and a variety of other patterns—adorn the bottoms of our footwear. (SICAR, the Shoeprint Image Capture and Retrieval System, contains more than 6,000 different sole patterns and is constantly adding more.) The fact that manufacturers strive to make their shoe and tire treads unique is a boon to crime scene investigators: this uniqueness makes tracing the suspect's print a much easier task.

Once a "known," or suspect, shoeprint is retrieved, investigators then compare it to the "unknown," or crime-scene, print. The comparison process is similar in many ways to the analysis performed on fingerprints. The investigator begins by comparing class characteristics—size, pattern, and manufacturer—and then moves on to individual characteristics. If the known print bears many or all of the same markings as the unknown, the investigator can confidently declare it a positive match.

Blood

Of all the types of evidence available for analysis, blood may be the most telling *and* the most incriminating. Centuries before the invention of reagents such as Luminol, poets and philosophers were well aware of the powerful symbolism of blood and its indelible nature. For instance, according to the Bible, it was the sound of his brother's blood crying out from the ground that incriminated Cain in the very first murder. And after killing the king, Shakespeare's murderous villain Macbeth anguished over the tenacious traces of blood that stained his hands. In another section of the castle, meanwhile, Lady Macbeth obsessed about that "damned spot" of blood that haunted her to the grave.

Bloodstain Pattern Analysis

Not only is blood difficult to get rid of, it's also extremely revealing. By studying the shape, size, and location of blood spatter, experts in blood-stain pattern analysis (BPA) can determine the sequence of events during and after a homicide. For example, BPA can indicate: the position of the victim at the time of an attack, the type of weapon used in the attack, the number of blows struck, and from which angles. Bloodstain patterns can also indicate whether the victim was dragged or moved after death.

The shape and size of blood drops are particularly telling to someone who knows how to read them. Large, circular drops on the ground, for instance, indicate that blood dripped passively from a source close to the ground. Smaller, "spattered" drops signify a forceful projection of blood, such as that resulting from a beating. In addition, the shape of the drops—elliptical or round—indicates the direction from which they originated.

Crime scenes often contain a variety of different blood spatter patterns, including cast-off stains, transfer or contact stains, blood smears or swipes, and blood pools. *Cast-off stains* are created when a bloodied weapon, such as a knife or a club, is swung through the air, flinging blood drops in a straight line up a wall and across the ceiling. *Transfer stains* result when a bloody surface touches an uncontaminated surface. For example, if someone steps in blood as he walks across the floor, he will leave behind transfer stains in the form of a trail of bloody footprints. *Blood smears* or *swipes* along a wall or floor may signify the attacker's movements or indicate whether or not a body has been moved. *Blood pools,* on the other hand, result when an injured person remains in one place for some time after being wounded. Once a person is dead he or she ceases to bleed, so if a pool of blood surrounds a body, it indicates the victim was stationary for a period of time prior to death.

Voids, or blank spaces, in the blood spatter also impart vital clues. A void suggests something (or someone) stood between the bleeder and the surface on which the blood spattered.

Finding Blood

Blood is one of the messiest elements a murderer must contend with if he attempts to cover his tracks. The human body contains approximately 1.5 gallons (5 l) of the sanguine fluid. During a violent attack, several pints can gush from wounds, spattering in all directions. Although the perpetrator may wipe up blatant puddles or sprays, he often overlooks stray drops and splatters that land behind doors, in cracks in the floors, or beneath furniture.

Even if the culprit does a perfect job of cleaning up, investigators have methods to expose dilute or occult blood (blood that is invisible to the naked eye). One method is to use reagents. These chemical substances react to and enhance the presence of blood and other bodily fluids. For instance, the reagent Luminol (sodium carbonate, sodium perborate, 3-aminothalhydrazide, and distilled water) causes the enzymes and iron in blood to luminesce, or glow, in the dark. Other reagents, such as Leucomalachite Green (leucomalachite, sodium perborate, and acetic acid) and Amido Black (Amido Black, glacial acetic acid, and methanol), also enhance dilute blood. Leucomalachite Green reacts with the hematin in blood and causes it to turn bright green; Amido Black turns it black. With these chemicals, it's possible for investigators to expose blood that is 10,000 times more dilute than the original.

Another means to discover dilute body

fluids at the crime scene is the use of the same light sources investigators use to seek out finger-prints. UV and ALS lights cause seminal stains and blood to fluoresce in the dark. So, although the perpetrator may feel confident he's washed away all traces of his presence, crime scene in-vestigators have the means to uncover them.

DNA

A hospital employee in the British village of Narborough, in Leicestershire, was on his way to work on the morning of November 22, 1983, when he stumbled across the lifeless body of 15-year-old Lynda Mann. The girl had been bru-tally raped and strangled, and her body left on the footpath next to a psychiatric hospital.

Although an intensive search of the area was conducted, the sole evidence discovered was seminal stains on the victim's clothing and body. The semen was tested using the only avail-able means at the time—a serological assay. All that the results revealed, however, was that the killer's semen was a rather rare type: it matched that of only 10 percent of the male population.

With no other clues and no suspects, the case went cold.

Over two years later, on July 31, 1986, the killer struck again. The body of 15-year-old Dawn Ashworth was discovered a short distance from the location of the first rape and murder. Once again, the only evidence investigators found was seminal fluid on the girl's body and clothing.

With little to go on, police focused their attention on all local males with records for sexual offences. One suspect, a young kitchen porter with a history of sexual assault, was brought in for questioning. Under pressure from the police, the porter promptly confessed to the murder but shortly afterward he retracted his confession.

At that point, police turned to Alec Jeffreys, a geneticist at the University of Leicester, for assistance in the investigation. Jeffreys had been working on a revolutionary new technique using DNA to accurately identify individuals. The police asked the geneticist to determine whether the same person had murdered both victims. They also wanted to know whether their suspect—the kitchen porter—was the guilty party.

The results were enlightening. The DNA test proved conclusively that both victims had indeed been raped and murdered by the same individual. That person, however, wasn't the kitchen porter.

Back at square one, the police appealed to the public. They requested that every male in the area submit a sample of blood for testing. Over 4,500 samples were tested before a positive match was made. The DNA of a 27-year-old baker by the name of Colin Pitchfork matched that found on the bodies of both girls.

In 1988, Pitchfork was found guilty of the murders and was sentenced to life in prison. He was the first person to be convicted based on DNA evidence. Since then, DNA typing, or "fingerprinting," has contributed profoundly to solving crime on both sides of the Atlantic.

DNA at the Crime Scene

In the 20 years since its inception, DNA typing has become so refined that today all that's required to produce a profile is a single drop of body fluid or an epithelial—a skin cell. At the crime scene, investigators seize drinking glasses, cigarette butts, chewing gum, or anything that may hold the perpetrator's body fluids or skin cells. In cases of sexual assault, mattresses and other areas where the assault may have occurred are thoroughly examined with UV lights for traces of blood, semen, and saliva. When discovered, dry blood and seminal stains are moistened with distilled water, swabbed, and packaged for delivery to a lab for processing.

The DNA Fingerprint

Strands of deoxyribonucleic acid (DNA), encoded with the blueprint that determines all of our individual characteristics, are coiled within the nucleus of our cells. These strands are wound together and form a double helix that makes up the 46 chromosomes found in all humans. Along with the genetic blueprint, there's also a great deal of what scientists refer to as "junk" on each of these strands. Because the "non-junk" is the same in all people, it's the junk DNA that is sampled to create the genetic fingerprint.

DNA is made up of chemical building blocks, or "base pairs," that are strung together. Junk DNA is made up of short sequences of the base pairs that repeat end to end. These are known as short tandem repeats (STRs). At certain points on the DNA strand, the arrangement of the STRs varies from one person to the next. By sampling the DNA at 13 of these points, geneticists can obtain a distinctive profile for each individual. How distinctive? Scientists maintain that the only people on earth who share the same DNA are identical twins.

In order to perform a DNA test, a certain

amount of genetic material is required. Often the DNA sample recovered from a crime scene is too minute to analyze. Therefore, in order to have a sufficient quantity for testing, the sample must first be amplified. This involves replicating the DNA through a chemical process known as polymerase chain reaction (PCR). During PCR, the original DNA sample serves as a template that is reproduced, or "photocopied," millions of times. The essential ingredients for amplification are the bases, primers, and enzymes. The primer for each type of STR is labeled with one of four colored fluorescent dyes. Once the DNA has been amplified, the specific STRs are separated by gel electrophoresis. During this process the STRs pass through a fluorescent dye detector. In the image that results, the STRs resemble a genetic barcode. This is the DNA fingerprint that is then analyzed by a technician and compared to the suspect's profile.

CODIS

In the early 1990s, the FBI began working on the Combined DNA Index System (CODIS). This interface serves as a search engine for all DNA databases available to investigators. Today, offenders convicted of sexual and violent crimes are required to submit a DNA sample. The profile from the offender's sample is then entered into a database. When DNA is recovered from a crime scene, investigators can compare this profile with all those in the system. This expedites the linking of violent crimes (such as rape and murder) to each other and to known convicted offenders.

Since the advent of CODIS, stories abound about suspects who

THE INNOCENCE PROJECT

The Innocence Project is an organization dedicated to seeing the wrongfully convicted exonerated through post-conviction DNA testing. Since its inception in 1992, the organization has helped exonerate over 160 wrongfully convicted persons. Furthermore, they report that as a consequence of DNA testing, hundreds of individuals are cleared before their cases go to trial each year.

are arrested for misdemeanors, such as shoplifting, only to have their DNA profile match that collected from an unsolved rape or murder. Dozens of cold cases have been solved thanks to CODIS. Just as importantly, dozens of wrongfully accused persons have been exonerated as a result of this computer technology.

Entomology

On one episode of *CSI*, lead investigator Gil Grissom finds a silphid beetle in an apartment abuzz with bluebottle flies. "The silphid beetle," he informs his partner, "feeds on decomposing flesh. Where there are silphids, there's a dead body." Grissom knows this because, well … he knows just about everything, it seems. What's more, he's a forensic entomologist.

Forensic entomology is the study of insects in connection with legal matters. The earliest known application of entomology in a criminal investigation occurred in 13th-century China. At that time, a forensic investigator was summoned to investigate a case in which a man had been murdered near a rice paddy. After examining the body and concluding that the victim had been stabbed to death, the investigator had all those who worked in the rice paddy bring their knives to the town square. There, he had each man place his knife on the ground in front of him. Before long, the murder weapon was crawling with blowflies, drawn by the scent of blood clinging to the knife. Confronted with this evidence, the killer broke down and confessed to the murder.

Today, forensic entomology is often used to establish time of death in homicide cases. It can also help determine whether or not a body was moved post mortem (from the Latin, meaning "after death"). And, occasionally, it can indicate whether or not poisoning was the cause of death.

Insects, such as blowflies and silphid beetles, are drawn to decomposing flesh. They feed on it, breed on it, and lay their eggs on it. The blowfly, in particular, has an amazing radar for death. Like vultures, blowflies often begin to appear on the scene minutes after death occurs. They lay their eggs around—and even inside—orifices and open wounds on the body. Then, between 12 and 48 hours after being laid, these eggs hatch into a squirming, insatiable army of maggots.

Maggots can remain on the corpse for periods lasting a week to two months, depending on ambient temperatures. During this time, they will devour every morsel of flesh until only cartilage and bone remain. Once the feast is over, the bloated maggots will seek out somewhere cool and dark to digest their meals and continue their development. Within 6–14 days, their metamorphosis is complete. After shedding their skin, they emerge as adult bluebottle or blowflies. The predictability of their behavior and the stages of development make these insects remarkably accurate indicators of the post mortem interval.

In order to determine time of death, the

forensic entomologist begins by collecting the larvae, or maggots, found on or near the victim's body. These are then taken back to the lab and reared until they metamorphose into adult flies. By recording the maggots' development, as well as the climatic conditions at the scene, the entomologist is able to pinpoint precisely when the first eggs were laid on the body. Consequently, the date and often the time of death are determined.

Firearms

There are many ways to kill a person. Poisoning, stabbing, shooting, drowning, burning, strangulation, and blunt-force trauma are a few of the more common methods employed by murderers. Some killers devise elaborate schemes to do away with their victims—others reach for the weapon nearest to hand.

In North America, guns are the murder weapons of choice. Of the 16,503 murders committed in the United States in 2003, the FBI estimates that 67 percent involved firearms, and of that percentage, most involved handguns. In comparison to knives, poison, ligatures, and other means and devices used in homicides, guns are quick, clean, accurate, and easily obtained. They do have a few drawbacks, however. Not only are they noisy, they also tend to leave a trail of evidence, including bullets, spent cartridges, and powder or gunshot residue.

When investigators arrive at the scene of a shooting, one of the first orders of business is to determine how many bullets were fired and where those bullets ended up. There are a variety of reasons for finding and collecting spent ammunition at the crime scene. First, these spent bullets and cartridges can help identify the caliber and make of the suspect weapon. In addition, finding the spent cartridges will give investigators an idea of the trajectory, or path, of the bullet. Knowing where shots originated can help recreate the scene. Moreover, once the suspect weapon is recovered, it must to the crime. To do this, investigators need the spent ammunition for comparison with test bullets fired from the recovered weapon. Therefore, recovering bullets and cartridges at a crime scene is a high priority.

Firearms come in a bewildering variety of shapes and sizes. There are rifles, revolvers, shotguns, and pistols. There are single-action, double-action, pump-action, bolt-action, lever-action, and hinged-action firearms. And there are semiautomatic and automatic weapons on the market today.

By the same token, there are literally hundreds of different kinds of ammunition available. But despite the wide variety, all ammunition shares certain characteristics. All ammunition has an outer casing (or cartridge) which contains gunpowder, a primer, and a projectile (bullet) or projectiles.

Likewise, all firearms—whether the gun is a handgun, a shotgun, or a rifle—work in a similar fashion. When the trigger is pulled, the firing pin discharges, strikes the primer, and ignites it. This, in turn, ignites the gunpowder contained in the cartridge, which expands and forces the bullet or projectile through the barrel and out of the muzzle. This firing process leaves a mechanical fingerprint on the ammunition. And like a human fingerprint, this mechanical imprint is entirely unique to the weapon that fires it.

Firearms Identification: Analysis and Comparison

Gun manufacturers all follow standardized specifications to produce the various makes and models of their weapons. Predictably, though, there are differences in the design standards of some makes and models. One significant characteristic is the rifling, which varies slightly from one manufacturer to the next.

Rifling is the arrangement of grooves that spiral along the inside of a gun barrel. These grooves, and the spaces between them, are known as *lands* and *grooves*. The function of the rifling is to put a spin on the bullet as it issues from the barrel of the gun. As any NFL quarterback knows, a spinning football flies farther and with greater precision than one without spin. This principle applies to any projectile, including bullets. Putting a spin on a bullet not only prevents it from wobbling in flight, it gives it much greater accuracy.

The rifling of some gun manufacturers, such as Colt, rotate to the left, while most others rotate to the right. In addition, the width and number of the lands and grooves differ from one manufacturer to another. This provides *striation evidence*—the markings impressed on the ammunition by the lands and grooves when the weapon is fired. Striation evidence enables investigators to identify the manufacturer and the type of weapon that fired the bullets recovered from a crime scene.

But striations from the lands and grooves aren't the only marks etched into the bullet as it spins through the barrel toward its intended target. It also picks up breech marks, firing pin impressions, extractor marks, and ejector marks, as well as tool marks from the machining process. Together, these scratches and impressions on the bullet's surface form the unique, complex signature of the specific weapon that fired it.

Once investigators recover the suspect weapon, it's sent to a lab for test firing and comparison testing. The gun is loaded and a round is fired into a tank of water or gel. The firearms analyst then compares the test bullet to the crime-scene bullet under a comparison microscope. If the striation evidence matches, investigators can be certain they've found their smoking gun.

Gunshot Residue

Often when a gun is fired, it leaks traces of antimony, barium, and lead from the primers that most cartridges contain. This is known as gunshot residue, or GSR. Although a shooter may not be aware of it, GSR often clings to his or her hands and clothing.

Therefore, if a suspect is apprehended early enough after firing a weapon, investigators can collect samples of GSR by swabbing the suspect's hands with a 5 percent nitrate solution, or with aluminum disks coated with a sticky substance. These samples are then analyzed using a scanning electron microscope.

However, GSR is extremely ephemeral and easily erased. If a suspect has washed or even wiped his or her hands since the shooting, all traces of GSR may be lost. In addition, not all weapons release residue when fired. So, while the presence of GSR on a suspect's hands can indicate guilt, its absence isn't necessarily an indication of innocence.

Post Mortem

As anyone who has watched an episode of *CSI, Law and Order*, or any other crime drama knows, a vital part of every homicide investigation is the post mortem. Until the medical examiner completes the autopsy, it's often difficult to determine the exact time and cause of death. And without this information, the chances of pinning down a suspect are minimal.

Therefore, whenever police are called to the scene of a sudden, unexpected, violent, or suspicious death, this medical–legal investigation is conducted. The ultimate goal of the post mortem is to establish three things: the time of death, the cause and manner of death, and, if necessary, the identity of the deceased.

The post mortem begins at the scene of the crime. Once notified that a body has been discovered, a deputy coroner, or death investigator, goes to the scene. This person's assessment at the scene is crucial to the case. Because the deputy coroner has paramedical training and sees more bodies in a month than most detectives see in a year, he or she can view the scene in an entirely different light than the detectives, noticing clues they might easily overlook.

One of the most important duties of the

deputy coroner is to check the body for three significant physiological changes that occur after death: *rigor mortis*, *algor mortis*, and lividity, or *livor mortis*. It's critical to the investigation that these changes are noted as early as possible.

The stiffening of the body, known as rigor mortis, or "rigor," begins to set in about two hours after death and follows a predictable pattern. The rigidity begins at the eyelids and lower jaw and moves steadily down toward the feet. Twelve hours after death the entire body is completely rigid, the limbs and torso frozen in whatever position they assumed at the time of death. The body remains in this state for another 12 hours. The process then begins to reverse, again starting at the head and moving downward. Thirty-six hours after death, all signs of rigor mortis will have vanished and the body will be limp once again. If a body is discovered at any point before or during rigor mortis, investigators can estimate time of death fairly accurately based on what stage it is in.

Another reliable indicator of time since death is algor mortis, or the internal temperature of the body. Immediately after death, the body's internal temperature, which is normally about 98.6° Fahrenheit (37° Celsius), begins to drop by one or two degrees an hour. Therefore, by taking the internal body temperature, investigators can estimate reasonably accurately how long it has been since death occurred.

The third post mortem physiological phenomenon forensic investigators look for is livor mortis, or lividity. Sometimes known as "the bruising of death," lividity is a distinct discoloration of the skin that begins to appear about two hours after death. The maroon-colored bruising is the result of blood pooling in the lowest extremities of the body. Once the heart stops beating, the blood stops circulating and succumbs to the pull of gravity, sinking to whatever part of the body happens to be closest to the ground. If a person dies while lying on his or her back, for example, the lividity will appear on the back.

Therefore, if a body is discovered face down, but lividity is apparent on the back side, this indicates that the body was moved post mortem.

Rigor mortis, algor mortis, and livor mortis are the tried and true signs of time of death. If these prove inconclusive, there still remain a few indicators investigators can rely on. One method is to sample the vitreous humor—the fluid in the eyeballs. After death, potassium is released during the breakdown of red blood cells, and this bleeds into the vitreous humor at a slow but steady rate. By measuring the amount of potassium in the eyeball fluid, the medical examiner can estimate with reasonable accuracy the time of death.

If a body isn't discovered for days, weeks, or months after death, the process of decomposition will be under way. Signs of decomposition include abdominal swelling, discoloration of the skin, and, last but certainly not least, the unmistakable, overwhelming odor. Experienced investigators are familiar with the various stages of decomposition and are frequently forced

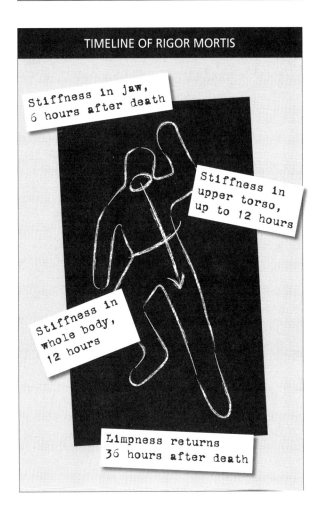

TIMELINE OF RIGOR MORTIS

Stiffness in jaw, 6 hours after death

Stiffness in upper torso, up to 12 hours

Stiffness in whole body, 12 hours

Limpness returns 36 hours after death

to rely on them for a rough estimate of the post-mortem interval.

Once the body has been carefully examined and photographed, and the deputy coroner has gleaned all of the information available at the scene, it is then readied for the trip to the morgue. First, the body is tagged for identification. Like every other piece of evidence collected at the crime scene, the body must also be accounted for at all times, and signed for each time it passes from the custody of one person to another. Hence the "toe tag." Once it has been tagged, and the hands and feet are enclosed in paper bags (to protect trace evidence such as gunshot residue or hair), the body is swaddled in a clean white sheet. Finally, the whole is placed in a body bag and taken to the morgue to be autopsied.

On *CSI*, autopsies are performed in a room with horror flick lighting, in a macabre atmosphere. Usually, only the medical examiner and one or two members of the investigative team are present for the procedure. Most real-life autopsies, on the other hand, are conducted in a well-lit operating room with several people in attendance. In addition to the medical examiner, often a forensic pathologist, the *diener* (or autopsy assistant), the detectives in charge of the case, the forensic photographer, and occasionally the district attorney—along with other forensic investigators such as anthropologists or entomologists—are present for the autopsy.

The post mortem is a multi-step process involving an intensive exterior and interior examination. The exterior examination begins with the removal of the fully clothed body from the body bag and placement on a stainless steel table. It is then thoroughly examined, photographed, weighed, and measured. Every detail—from hair and eye color to rips, tears, or cuts in the clothing—is noted. After this initial examination is complete, the clothing is removed and placed in paper bags to be sent to the lab for trace evidence analysis.

Once nude, the body is again photographed in detail. Special attention is paid to any scars, bruises, birthmarks, and tattoos, or "tats," which might serve to identify the victim or the killer. Fingernail scrapings and mouth and anal swabs are taken for DNA analysis. Samples of hair are plucked from the head and pubic area. The entire body is then examined for trace evidence—hairs, fibers, glass fragments, dirt, and any other materials. If a sexual attack is suspected, the medical examiner scrutinizes the body with a UV or ALS light for traces of seminal fluids.

Some homicides can easily be misinterpreted as suicides or accidents. Drowning and burning deaths, in particular, can be problematic for investigators. Killers will often try to conceal their crimes by setting a building on fire or by tossing the body into a lake, river, or the ocean, making the death appear to be an accident or suicide. The medical examiner must therefore be alert to indications of foul play.

Once the external examination of the body

is complete, the investigative process becomes graphic. The medical examiner begins the internal autopsy by opening the body with a "Y" incision. This gash exposes the chest plate and liver and the large and small intestines in one precise maneuver. After opening the body cavity, the medical examiner scrutinizes each organ *in situ*. Then, one by one, the organs are removed from the body and weighed. During this phase of the autopsy, bodily fluids are also drawn and sent to toxicology for analysis. The stomach is removed and its contents analyzed.

Although a rather nasty task, analyzing the stomach contents can bring to light some fairly significant clues, such as what, when, and even where the victim ate last. This information can help establish the individual's activities prior to death. More importantly, the analysis can reveal whether or not the cause of death was due to drug overdose or poisoning.

The final step in the autopsy is to remove and analyze the brain. This involves peeling back the scalp and cutting through the top of the skull. Before sectioning the brain for analysis, the medical examiner weighs and examines it thoroughly for signs of trauma.

Ideally, once the autopsy is complete, the medical examiner will be able to inform detectives about the cause of death, the type of weapon used, and provide an assortment of vital information pertaining to the case. Armed with this knowledge, investigators can hit the streets with a better understanding of who and what it is they're looking for.

Identifying the Victim

Killers often go to great lengths to disguise the identity of their victims. For example, the victims of mob- or drug-related homicides frequently have their hands and feet removed and disposed of elsewhere, so they can't be identified by fingerprint records. In such cases, and to facilitate the identity of a suspect, detectives must first establish the victim's identity.

One of the most extreme cases of a killer's efforts to erase all traces of his victims' identities occurred in England in the late 1940s. At that time, con man John George Haigh preyed on wealthy single women, whom he seduced with his good looks and charm. Once he'd swindled the women out of their fortunes, Haigh killed them and disposed of the bodies by dumping them in a vat of acid.

The con man was confident that without a body, police couldn't charge him with murder. He was so confident of this, in fact, that after killing Olive Durand-Beacon and giving her the acid bath treatment, Haigh openly bragged about the murder. When police got wind of this, they raided his workshop. There they discovered several barrels of sludge, which they carted off to the forensic pathologist's lab. The contents of the barrels were analyzed and found to contain traces of human fat, gallstones, and a set of dentures. Based on this evidence, Haigh was tried and convicted for the murder of Olive Durand-Beacon.

* * *

If a body has decayed to the extent that only a skeleton remains when it's discovered, identification can be problematic. In these cases, forensic anthropologists are often consulted.

For those who know how to read them, bones can be very illuminating. By examining a skeleton, forensic anthropologists often determine the victim's sex, age, build, and ethnicity. On occasion, they can even deduce the cause of death.

Sex is established by analyzing the skull and hips. Males have a narrower sacrum and hips than do females. The skull reveals ethnicity: Mongoloid, Negroid, and Caucasoid skulls each have distinctive characteristics. Approximate age can be established by examining the size of the bones. Another good indication of age is the amount of decay and wear and tear bones have suffered. In older victims, signs of deterioration occur in the teeth, joints, and vertebrae.

Victims can also be identified by searching for known fractures on the remains. Although broken bones heal eventually, visible reminders of the fractures always remain.

Forensic anthropologists can also determine the cause of death in many cases. Violence invariably leaves visible marks, no matter how old the skeleton. Bullet holes in skulls or bones are obvious. A knife can also leave a mark, if the blade scrapes a rib or penetrates a bone. And blunt force trauma is evident in shattered bones and fractured skulls.

So, no matter what actions a killer takes to cover his tracks, or how cold the case may be, if a trace of evidence exists, forensic investigators have the means and methods to unearth crucial information to eventually solve the crime.

Case Studies

CHAPTER 3

All Arches

It wasn't like Helen* to go so long without calling home. Ever since she moved halfway across the country to Moncton, New Brunswick, she had made it a point to call her father on a regular basis. John Muir* looked forward to these calls. Hearing his daughter's voice once a week was reassuring; it helped ease his concerns about her being so far away. But it had now been

---

* Names have been changed

well over a month since he'd heard from her. She'd never gone that long before without calling. Muir sensed something was terribly wrong.

The fact that Helen worked as an exotic dancer had always worried John Muir. It was a hazardous profession. He knew all too well that women like Helen frequently disappeared, never to be heard from again. After two weeks had passed without a call, he began calling her. He'd dialed her number dozens of times and left several messages, each one more frantic than the last. When he finally managed to reach her boyfriend, Kurt Anderson*, Muir's worries only escalated. Anderson reported that he and Helen had quarreled. She'd packed her bags and left town. That was all he knew.

Muir felt certain Anderson was lying. After hanging up, he decided it was time to call the police.

---

* Name has been changed

To the investigators of the Codiac detachment of the RCMP in Moncton, this appeared to be a routine missing persons case. They began by questioning Helen Muir's neighbors and co-workers about her whereabouts. The girls at the club where she worked said they hadn't seen Helen for several weeks. This wasn't too unusual, though. In their business, women came and went all the time. They'd drift into town, work for a while, and then move on. A couple of the girls did recall that Helen had been having a rough time with her boyfriend. Perhaps she'd left town to escape a sour relationship.

A check into Helen's cell phone and credit card records revealed that both had been used recently. This didn't really prove anything though: anyone could be using the cards and cell phone. A red flag went up, however, when police checked with the power company and discovered the hydro at Helen's residence on Archibald Street had been disconnected. The accounts person at NB Power informed RCMP investigators that the reason given for the disconnection was that the customer, Helen Muir, was deceased.

By that time, Kurt Anderson had been under surveillance for a few days. The slightly built, 27-year-old had a previous record for petty offences, but he wasn't "well known" to police. Anderson had already taken up with a new woman and the two had moved into a house in Memramcook, a small community about 20 minutes southeast of Moncton. When a friend who had helped Anderson move was questioned by the detectives, another red flag was raised. During the interview, the friend let it slip that Anderson had moved most of Helen's furniture to his new place.

Although they still had no proof that this was anything more than a routine missing persons case, investigators began to suspect foul play. They decided to ask Corporal Paula Dionne, the forensic identification specialist in Moncton, to join the investigation. They also applied for a warrant to search Helen Muir's house.

* * *

It was obvious that the dilapidated, two-story house on Archibald Street had recently been vacated. Most of the furniture was gone. Just a few ratty pieces remained in the empty rooms. Garbage littered the floors and dust had collected in the corners. As Dionne and the others poked around in the frigid, vacant house, they came across what appeared to be bloodstains on a door leading into the kitchen. This prompted them to call Staff Sergeant Neil Fraser, the blood spatter pattern analysis expert with the RCMP's Regional Forensic Identification Services in Halifax, Nova Scotia.

The sun was already low in the sky by the time Fraser arrived in Moncton on February 15, 1999. After 25 years on the force, Fraser's passion for the job had never wavered. Solving crimes was all he'd ever wanted to do in life, and even after all these years he still approached each case with the enthusiasm of a rookie.

When Corporal Dionne led him into the

kitchen and pointed out the stain on the door, Fraser was pretty sure it wasn't blood. A quick presumptive test with a strip of Hemastix (small strips used by doctors to test for blood in urine) confirmed his suspicions. If the stain had been blood, the Hemastix would have turned a dark green color. However, it remained unchanged.

After examining the stain, Fraser and Dionne did a walk-through. Fraser remarked on the excessive amount of dust and grime throughout the house. In his experience, this wasn't consistent with the cleaning up of a bloody scene. If there had been a lot of blood around and someone had attempted to clean it up, they would have inadvertently removed some of the dust and grime as well.

While the investigators were in the midst of their walk-through, a warrant to search Anderson's new residence came through. Leaving Dionne and Fraser to continue their search, the other investigators headed to Memramcook.

After completing their tour of the upper

part of the house, Fraser and Dionne went down to the basement. The cramped, dimly lit space was unfinished and had a rough concrete floor. A small workshop at the bottom of the stairs caught their attention, but it was too dark to see much of anything. After a quick look around, they decided they'd need more light before continuing the search.

Just then, one of the investigators at the Anderson residence called. They'd made a big find, he informed them. "You'd better get over here right away," he said.

By the time Fraser and Dionne arrived in Memramcook, it was well past midnight. However, they had no trouble finding the house. Every light in the place was blazing. A ribbon of yellow crime-scene tape surrounded the property, and several cruisers were parked out front.

The file coordinator for the scene met them at the door and filled them in on what had happened. Shortly after beginning their search of Anderson's residence, the investigators made a gruesome discovery. In the shed out back they found a large duffle bag. Inside the outer bag was a second bag. Inside that was something wrapped in several layers of transparent plastic. The plastic was smeared with what appeared to be blood. The weight and size of the bag suggested there could be a body inside, but until they pulled out the contents they couldn't be certain. If it was a body, the investigators didn't want to risk contaminating any evidence by pulling it from the duffle. The best way to handle it, they decided, was to send the bag straight to the morgue in Saint John.

After cautiously examining and photographing the duffle bag, the investigators placed it in a body bag and sent it to the morgue. Fraser and Dionne then began a walk-through of the Memramcook house. At that point, they had no idea if the murder had occurred there or at the house in Moncton. Nor did they have any idea how the victim (if there was one) had died. So it was difficult to know exactly what to look for.

However, when the two reached the basement, it became clear that although the victim may not have died in the Memramcook house, her killer had obviously intended to bury her there.

The dirt floor of the basement had originally been covered with a layer of crushed gravel. Near the furnace, the gravel had been pushed off to one side. There, someone had dug a hole approximately four feet deep, three and a half feet wide, and five feet long. The investigators had been lucky: if they'd waited a day or two before entering the house, the body would already have been buried and the fresh grave recovered with gravel. No one, except the killer, would have known it was there.

After completing their search of the basement, Fraser and Dionne returned to the kitchen. Although they had discovered the intended grave, they had yet to determine where the murder had occurred. As Fraser glanced around the room, a drop of blood on the back of one of the chrome and vinyl chairs caught his attention. The chrome kitchen set, Dionne told him, would have been moved from the Archibald Street house within the past week or so. After 13 years in Ident, Fraser knew that where there's one spot of blood, there are bound to be more. He flipped the chair over and found the whole underside to be covered with projected blood spatter.

By now, the post mortem was just getting under way in Saint John. Eric Mullins and Bob Hart, two investigators working on the case, attended the autopsy. They would answer any questions the medical examiner had about the scene, as well as report back to the team when anything unusual or important cropped up.

As the contents of the duffel bag were cautiously lifted out and placed on the stainless steel table beneath the harsh lights, a hush fell in the room. The body was wrapped in a Canadian flag and several layers of plastic that were bound with duct tape. The medical examiner carefully peeled off the plastic and the flag one layer at a time. These were then placed in evidence bags; they would later be scrutinized for trace evidence at the forensics lab.

The victim was folded into a fetal position. Her wrists and ankles were bound with silver duct tape and a black garbage bag covered her head. When the bag was removed, they saw she had been badly beaten. Blood matted her hair, and her face was bruised and swollen.

During the external examination of the body, the medical examiner found traces of a black, waxy substance on the victim's buttocks. Knowing this was critical evidence, Mullins called Fraser to ask if he'd come across anything matching this description in their search. At the mention of the wax, Fraser remembered seeing a black candle sitting on the floor of the basement in the house on Archibald Street.

Since they'd finished their search of the Memramcook house by then, Fraser and Dionne returned to Archibald Street. There, they headed straight for the basement and began scouring for evidence that would confirm this was where the murder had been committed. It wasn't long before they found what they were looking for. Just as Fraser had recalled, a large, half-melted black candle sat off in one corner. Near the candle, he noticed what appeared to be blood spatter on the floor. As he shone his flashlight around, more blood spatter became apparent. Blood was sprayed across the cover of the power panel, a beam on the ceiling, and the water heater. Clearly a brutal attack had occurred in that area recently.

Fraser noted that the blood spatter on the water heater and beams was consistent with cast-off stains. Apparently the killer had repeatedly swung a bloodied object overhead, such as a hammer or knife, during the attack. As he looked around, Fraser discovered another important clue. At the center of the blood spatter on the floor was a large, rectangular-shaped void. On closer inspection, he noticed that the angle of the projected bloodstains at the edges of this void indicated they originated from the void's center. It appeared that Helen Muir's killer had dragged her down to the basement, spread the sheet of plastic out on the floor, and then proceeded to beat her to death on top of it.

After they'd completed their search, Dionne set up the lights and camera and photographed the scene in detail while Fraser took swabs from each of the bloodstained areas for DNA testing. Investigators rely on their own judgment when collecting samples. If they feel there may have been more than one bleeder at the scene, more samples are collected. If it appears that there was only one bleeder, they take a sample from each area where blood is discovered. Whether or not all the samples get tested depends on what information emerges during the investigation.

When Fraser and Dionne were about to pack up and head to the lab, Mullins called to report that the autopsy was finished. The medical examiner's conclusions confirmed Fraser's suspicions. Helen Muir had died of injuries caused by blunt force trauma. Despite an extensive search of both residences, however, the weapon was never recovered.

Back at the Moncton lab, the plastic the body had been wrapped in was placed in the fuming chamber and exposed to super glue fumes. When heated, super glue vapors bond with the residue of fingerprints and turn them an opaque white. The investigators' efforts were rewarded when several perfect prints materialized. Good prints are rare. Rarer still are prints with predominately arch patterns, the least common of the friction ridge patterns. Only five percent of the population has all arch fingerprints, and Kurt Anderson was among that five percent. Sure enough, when Anderson's prints were compared to those from the crime scene, they proved a positive match.

Although the murder weapon was never found, the prosecution had sufficient evidence to bring a first-degree murder charge against Anderson for the beating death of Helen Muir.

At the trial, the prosecutor pointed out the fact that Anderson's fingerprints were discovered on the plastic in which the body was wrapped, as well as the duct tape used to seal it. The fingerprints, in addition to the freshly dug grave in his basement and Helen Muir's body in his shed, were highly incriminating. Then there was also the black wax found on the victim's body, which matched that of the candle found in the basement of the Archibald Street house. Each of these items implicated Anderson in the murder. The void in the blood spatter in the basement of the Archibald Street house, however, implied premeditation.

Although nothing could ease John Muir's grief over the loss of his daughter, at least seeing her killer brought to justice provided a sense of closure. Kurt Anderson was convicted of first-degree murder and sentenced to 14 years in prison.

CHAPTER 4

#263—L, Eugene, Ore.

When Chief Agent Dan O'Connell arrived at railroad Tunnel No. 13 in the Siskiyou Mountains of Southern Oregon, he discovered a scene that had all the hallmarks of an amateur heist gone tragically wrong. On the afternoon of October 11, 1923, the Gold Special, a train rumored to be carrying nearly half a million dollars, had entered the 3,107-foot (947 m) tunnel. It never emerged.

An explosion had rocked the train, and

the bodies of four men were scattered in and around the cars. Engineer Sidney Bates, brakeman Coyle Johnson, and fireman Marvin Seng had all been shot to death. The fourth victim, Elvyn Dougherty, the mail clerk, had perished in the explosion. It appeared that the would-be train robbers had attempted to blast the doors off the mail car to access the precious cargo. However, their plan had gone awry. Rather than just blasting off the doors, the explosion had ripped the car apart and sparked a blazing fire. The searing heat and blinding smoke prevented the robbers from entering the mail car. Stymied, they fled the scene empty handed.

As Dan O'Connell and his team sifted through the wreckage at the crime scene, they discovered a revolver, the detonator for the explosives, and some pieces of creosote-soaked jute sacking. The sacking, the investigator figured, was meant to cover the perpetrators' shoes in order to throw off the tracking dogs. The team also turned up a pair of worn, stained overalls.

The evidence looked promising. O'Connell was certain they would soon crack the case.

While the evidence was being analyzed, dozens of police, railway employees, state troopers, and tracking dogs combed the rugged mountain terrain for any sign of the killers. Nevertheless, the suspects somehow evaded capture. To make matters worse, the evidence yielded little in the way of clues. Before long, the trail went cold. In desperation, O'Connell turned to noted criminalist Edward O. Heinrich for help.

At 42, Heinrich had established a solid reputation as a first-rate forensic investigator. He had worked on investigations all over the country, including the infamous Fatty Arbuckle manslaughter case. He was known as "the Sherlock Holmes of America."

After examining the other evidence, Heinrich turned his attention to the overalls. To his trained eye, every stain, every frayed and worn area, and every tuft of lint from the pockets told a story.

O'Connell was astonished when Heinrich reported back to him a few days later with a detailed profile of the suspect. The man O'Connell sought, Heinrich informed him, was a left-handed lumberjack from the Pacific Northwest. He was approximately 5 foot 10, weighed 165 pounds, had light brown hair, and was a smoker.

How had Heinrich gleaned all this information from a dirty, old pair of overalls? Their size, of course, gave him an idea of the suspect's height and weight. And from the wear around the pockets and the fact that the overalls had been buttoned from the left, he deduced that the man was left-handed. A light brown hair, which Heinrich presumed belonged to the owner of the overalls, was discovered on one of the buttons. The trace evidence pulled from the pockets added more details to the portrait. Buried among the lint, he'd found fragments of cigarette tobacco and chips of Douglas fir, a tree that was indigenous to the Northwest. This, along with pine pitch staining the overalls, suggested the suspect was a lumberjack who smoked cigarettes.

But this wasn't all Heinrich discovered during his analysis. Jammed in the bottom of one of the pockets he found a crumpled, faded piece of paper that had been overlooked by O'Connell. This would prove to be the Rosetta stone of the case.

The slip of paper had been shoved into the pocket and forgotten by the owner. It had been washed at least once with the overalls, rendering the printing on it almost completely illegible. After examining it under a high-powered microscope, Heinrich exposed the paper to iodine fumes—a technique used to reveal latent fingerprints on porous materials. Although no prints showed up, the code #263—L, Eugene Ore. appeared. The paper, O'Connell would discover, was a registered mail receipt issued at Eugene, Oregon.

The number on the receipt was eventually traced to 23-year-old Roy d'Autremont, a left-handed lumberjack from Eugene. When police conducted a background check on Roy, they discovered he had two brothers—a twin named Ray, and a 19-year-old brother named Hugh. All three brothers had been missing since the day of the botched robbery of the Gold Special.

The ensuing manhunt for the d'Autremont brothers was one of the largest in U.S. history. For three and a half years, police searched in vain for the siblings. Wanted posters of Roy, Ray, and Hugh were distributed to police departments worldwide. But lead after lead generated nothing of note. Then, one day, a sergeant in the U.S. army who had just returned from the Philippines identified Hugh. The youngest of the d'Autremont brothers had been serving in the 31st infantry in the Philippines under an assumed name.

In February 1927, Hugh d'Autremont was arrested and returned to Oregon to stand trial for murder. On June 21, he was found guilty and sentenced to life in prison for his part in the murders of the four men on the Gold Special.

While Hugh's trial was in progress, the twins were discovered in Steubenville, Ohio, where they had been working in a steel mill under assumed identities. Faced with the damning evidence held by prosecutors, and paired with the fact that Hugh had been found guilty, Ray and Roy decided to plead guilty and were also sentenced to life in prison.

CHAPTER 5

Helle Crafts

It was before dawn on a cold, blustery November morning when *au pair* Marie Thomas was awakened by her boss, Richard Crafts. A severe winter storm had been raging throughout the night, and the power was off throughout the Crafts' neighborhood in Newtown, Connecticut. Crafts told Marie to get the children up and dressed. He explained that his wife, Helle, was on her way to his sister's place in Westport, and they were all to meet up with her there shortly.

The 19-year-old was puzzled about the rush to get to Westport. After all, it was only 6 a.m. and driving conditions were treacherous that morning. She knew better than to question Crafts, though. In the few months she had been working for him, she'd come to realize he was a moody and unpredictable character who often lashed out at his wife and children for no good reason. After rousing the children from their slumber, Marie hurried them into their clothes and out to the car.

It turned out Helle Crafts wasn't waiting for them at her sister-in-law's as Richard said she would be. In fact, the 39-year-old flight attendant was never seen alive again.

Twelve days later, on December 1, 1986, private investigator Keith Mayo called the Newtown Police Department to report that his client, Helle Crafts, was missing. Moreover, he feared her husband, Richard, might have murdered her.

At first, police didn't take Mayo's statement or the missing persons case very seriously. They knew Richard Crafts well. In fact, until recently, the Eastern Airline pilot had been an auxiliary member of their force. Sure, Richard was a little eccentric. Many of them felt it was peculiar that a highly paid airline pilot with a beautiful wife and three young children would spend all his spare time hanging around the police station and responding to calls. And they'd all heard rumors about the Crafts' tumultuous relationship. Richard didn't even try to hide the fact that he cheated on his wife. Helle, on the other hand, often tried to conceal bruises and black eyes behind makeup and dark glasses.

Still, there was no evidence of murder. Perhaps Helle had decided she'd had enough of her husband's philandering and abuse and had taken off. As a flight attendant with Pan Am, she could easily have hopped on a flight to Denmark to visit her ailing mother, as Richard claimed she had. The fact that her Toyota Tercel had been found in the Pan Am employee parking lot at JFK airport seemed to substantiate this claim.

However, Richard Crafts had presented half a dozen different excuses to as many people about his wife's disappearance. Also troublesome was the fact that Helle had recently retained a divorce lawyer, as well as the private investigator. She'd hinted to friends that she feared for her life. "If anything happens to me," she told one close friend, "don't assume it was an accident."

Even so, when police checked into the matter, they found no solid evidence of foul play. Perhaps Mayo was worrying needlessly. Missing spouses often showed up alive and well sooner or later. The Newtown police were betting that's what would happen in this case.

When Richard, Marie, and the children arrived at his sister's place in Westport that wintry November morning, he seemed distracted. After a short time, he made an excuse about having to go home to check on something. He told Marie he would return before long to retrieve her and the children. But he didn't return until nine o'clock that evening. On the drive back to Newtown, Marie noticed that Richard seemed exhausted. He was so exhausted, in fact, that she was concerned he would fall asleep at the wheel.

A few days later, the au pair observed some dark stains on the rug in the master bedroom. When she asked Richard about them, he said he'd spilled kerosene on the carpet. The next day, Marie was surprised to see that the stained portion of the carpet had been torn up. A few days later, when detectives questioned him about the missing carpet, Richard stated that the blue wall-to-wall carpeting throughout the house needed to be replaced. It was easier to tear it up in small chunks, he explained, than try to take it all up at once.

The police appeared to be satisfied with this explanation, but Keith Mayo wasn't. Convinced the carpet was crucial evidence, and that what had been spilled on it was probably not kerosene but his missing client's blood, he tracked down the waste management facility where the town's garbage was disposed. He then recruited a search party to help find the evidence.

For the next few days, he and his recruits pawed through partially frozen peaks and valleys of reeking trash in the Canterbury Dump, in search of the chunk of stained carpeting. Finally, when continuing their slog through the stinking morass seemed pointless, a triumphant whoop arose as a piece of blue carpeting was pulled from the debris.

The carpet remnant was rushed to the state police lab for analysis. Mayo waited anxiously for the results. To that point, other than questioning Richard, the police had done little to find Mayo's missing client. If the stains proved to be blood, he felt certain they would be forced to take the case seriously.

It was a blow to the private investigator when the results came back negative. However, this didn't deter his quest for justice.

By then the media had caught wind of Helle

Crafts' disappearance. In a story in the *Danbury Times* on December 17, Mayo slammed the Newtown police for their lack of action on the case. At the same time, Helle's friends began to demand the case be considered critical. The willowy blonde was the type who inspired devotion in her numerous friends, and those friends were growing irate that nothing had been done about her disappearance. In fact, it appeared that no one other than Keith Mayo seemed to be taking it seriously.

Everyone who knew her was aware Helle was a loving, devoted mother. Her friends protested that she would never have abandoned her children willingly. There was also the fact that Helle had been considering putting an end to her unhappy marriage. Despite the reality that Richard had been unfaithful to her from the start, he wasn't willing to let her go. There was growing suspicion among Helle's closest friends that she and Richard had fought over the divorce and that he had flown into a rage and killed her. It seemed a likely explanation for her disappearance.

Concerned about the public's growing dissatisfaction with the Newtown PD's handling of the case, the state attorney's office stepped in and turned it over to the Western District's Major Crimes Unit.

After some preliminary investigation, the detectives working the case felt there was sufficient probable cause to secure a warrant to search the Crafts' residence at 5 Newfield Lane. The warrant came through on Christmas Day. Luckily, Richard happened to be away at the time. Wanting to escape the constant scrutiny he'd been subject to since his wife's disappearance, he decided to pack up the children and head to his mother's place in Florida for the holidays.

Although they would rather have been home eating Christmas dinner with their families, Henry Lee, chief criminalist and director of the Connecticut State Police Lab, and a team of detectives and crime scene investigators rendezvoused at the gray-shingled, ranch-style house on Newfield Lane that afternoon.

At that time, Lee had been in law enforcement for 30 years. He'd started out in the Taiwan Central Police College in 1956 and, after a stint with the Taiwan PD, went on to complete a degree in forensic science at John Jay College of Criminal Justice and a PhD in biochemistry at New York University. Lee's dedication and attention to detail were legendary. For the next few months, this investigation would occupy his every waking hour.

In the scenic, little village of Newtown, the Crafts' house was unquestionably an eyesore. As a highly paid airline pilot, Richard had a sizeable disposable income. However, most of it was spent on toys for himself and not on the house's upkeep. The yard was littered with an assortment of broken and rusting machinery, and the house itself was in total disrepair. It seemed Richard had priorities other than maintaining appearances.

Inside the house, the same level of squa-
lor prevailed. It appeared that in the weeks
since his wife's disappearance, Richard Crafts
had been busy. The carpets had all been torn
up and removed. Mattresses had been dragged
from the children's bedrooms and deposited
on the floor in the master bedroom. Children's
toys, dirty laundry, and dirty dishes were strewn
throughout the house. The place had the look of
a temporary encampment on the front lines of
turmoil. The arsenal of weapons investigators
found stashed in the basement only served to
reinforce this perception.

A gun fanatic, Crafts had collected enough
weapons to equip a small army. During their
search, investigators tagged and bagged an astonishing assortment of guns and ammunition,
including Smith and Wesson revolvers, Ruger
carbine rifles, semiautomatic weapons, Beretta
handguns, crossbows, shotguns, rifles, as well
as grenades.

Over the next few days, Lee and his team

combed the entire house for evidence. The investigators worked in pairs, with each pair assigned to a particular segment of the house. In addition to the cache of weapons, they found and seized bloody towels and bedding. When they sprayed Luminol around the master bedroom, blood spatter appeared in patterns consistent with a vicious attack. Despite the volume of evidence discovered at 5 Newfield Lane, however, investigators still had no body and no solid evidence that Helle Crafts wasn't still alive. In short, they had no case.

The frustrated investigators returned to scrutinizing Richard's activities in the weeks prior to Helle's disappearance. A check of his credit card purchases turned up two interesting items. One was the recent acquisition of a full-sized Westinghouse Freezer, which was conspicuously absent from the Crafts residence at the time of the search. The other was a rental charge of $900 for equipment from Darien Rentals. Unable to surmise what kind of equipment rental would be so costly, the detectives paid Darien Rentals a visit. The charge, it turned out, was for a Bush Bandit—one of the most heavy-duty wood chippers available.

After the discovery of the Bush Bandit rental, detectives interviewed snowplow driver Joseph Hine. Hine was plowing River Road on the night of November 20, he told them, when he noticed a U-Haul truck with a large wood chipper attached to it by the side of the road near the intersection of South Flat Hill Rd. As Hine approached, he noticed a man standing beside the truck. When he slowed down, the man waved him on. That was at 3:30 a.m. It was an odd time, Hine thought, to be out chipping wood in the midst of a blizzard.

After the interview, Hine led detectives to the area where he had encountered the wood chipper that night. It was outside Southbury, on the shores of the Housatonic River. Detectives Patrick McCafferty and T. K. Brown scouted around the area and soon came across several mounds of woodchips on the banks of the river. As they examined the debris, they noticed bits of shredded paper and green plastic—of the type used for green garbage bags—among the woodchips. As Brown poked around among the debris, he came across what would prove a pivotal piece of evidence—a soggy, stained envelope. The name and address printed on the envelope were still legible: Helle L. Crafts, 5 Newfield Lane, Newtown, Connecticut.

Suddenly, the investigation that had taken so long to sputter to a start kicked into high gear. Before long, the scene was secured and dozens of investigators began the painstaking process of combing the area in search of evidence. As the mounds of woodchips were methodically sorted, the gruesome reality of Helle Crafts' fate became clear. Several strands of long, blonde hair, clothing fibers, and bone fragments were unearthed. This, and all other evidence, including the woodchips, was photographed, bagged, tagged, and transported to the lab for analysis.

While the intense search on the shore of the Housatonic River continued, the Bush Bandit Richard Crafts had rented was seized and hauled to the lab. There, every surface of the machine was inspected for fingerprints, blood, and any trace evidence it might hold.

As the riverbank search continued, investigators speculated that Richard Crafts had backed the wood chipper up to the bank and fed his wife's body into the machine one piece at a time with the intention of tossing all the evidence into the river's swift current. If this was so, then what they were discovering on the banks was only a fragment of the whole. The majority of Helle Crafts' remains were likely at the bottom of the Housatonic River.

Divers were called in to search the riverbed. Because the water was so icy, they could only stay submerged a few minutes at a time, which made the task extremely arduous. Furthermore, the water's murkiness prevented them from seeing beyond a few feet. Despite these difficulties, the team persevered.

After two weeks of intensive searching, they had recovered several pieces of crucial evidence. One of the largest finds was a Stihl chainsaw. Many bits and pieces of a human body were also discovered, including part of a toe, a small portion of a finger, two teeth—one with a portion of the jawbone attached—a piece of skull, dozens of bone fragments, and hundreds of blond hairs.

Lee had his staff of 28 work around the clock on the case. He also recruited several forensic experts to help with the investigation, including, forensic odontologist Gus Karazulas. When he analyzed the teeth found in the river, Karazulas ascertained that one of the recovered teeth matched Helle Crafts' lower left bicuspid.

The chainsaw chain also proved extremely probative. When it was pulled from the water, investigators noticed that its serial number had been filed off. Using acid etching, they were able to restore the number. The chainsaw, it was determined, had been purchased in 1981 by Richard Crafts. Snared in its teeth were several blue fibers that matched the rug from the Crafts' residence, as well as blond hair and fragments of human flesh.

Lee labored tirelessly over the bone fragments and woodchips. Eventually, he was able to prove that the marks on each substance matched. Whatever had created the woodchips had also created the bone fragments. This, he later testified, was an extremely heavy-duty piece of equipment.

Finally, on January 13, 1987, Richard Crafts was arrested and charged with the murder of his wife, Helle. Investigators had spent innumerable hours collecting, analyzing, and compiling the evidence. The prosecution knew, though, that without a body it would be a tough case to win. By the time the trial commenced in March 1988, State Attorney Walter Flanagan had lined up an impressive array of witnesses and felt confident about his case. Nevertheless, after three months, the trial terminated with a hung jury, and a mistrial was declared. Richard Crafts walked out of the courthouse a free man.

The embattled killer didn't remain at liberty for long. In March 1989, a second trial got under way. This time the jury was unanimous in its decision: Richard Crafts was found guilty of the brutal slaying of his wife and sentenced to 99 years in prison.

For Lee and his team of forensic investigators, the conviction of Richard Crafts vindicated their efforts and the countless hours spend laboring under intensely difficult conditions to retrieve and analyze the grisly evidence.

CHAPTER 6

Robert Fisher: FBI's Most Wanted

The morning shift was just getting started at the Scottsdale PD in Arizona on April 10, 2001, when a call came in reporting an explosion and fire at the suburban home of Robert and Mary Fisher. When firefighters eventually extinguished the blaze, a few scorched walls were all that was left of the house. When the site had cooled enough for investigators to begin processing the scene, they made a horrific discovery. Among the charred ruins were the bodies of a woman and two children. These, they presumed, were the remains of Mary Fisher, her 12-year-old daughter, Brittany, and 10-year-old son, Bobby Jr.

The autopsies concluded that the victims had not died as a result of the fire. Mary had been shot once in the back of the head and her throat had been slit. Both the children's throats had also been slit prior to the explosion. Clearly, the killer had staged the blast and consequent fire in an attempt to cover his tracks.

Because there had been an explosion, members of the U.S. Department of Justice's Bureau of Alcohol, Tobacco, Firearms, and Explosives (ATF) and local arson investigators, along with a specially trained dog, scoured the crime scene for traces of explosives. None were found. Instead, authorities discovered the blast was the result of the intentional disconnection of the oil furnace from its fuel line. Not far from the disconnected line sat an incendiary device. In addition, the burn pattern and fumes indicated the killer had liberally splashed accelerants throughout the bedrooms and over the bodies.

As detectives canvassed the neighborhood, they learned that the Fishers owned a dog named Blue. There was no sign, however, of either Robert Fisher or Blue anywhere. Mary's SUV was also missing. It appeared that Fisher had brutally murdered his wife and children in their sleep the night before, and had then rigged the house to explode once he'd made his getaway.

The first 48 hours of any homicide investigation are critical. In order to pin down a suspect and solve the case, everyone involved works overtime during those first two days—running down leads and searching for evidence before the trail goes cold. Anxious to catch the perpetrator of this heinous crime, the Scottsdale PD threw all of their resources into the Fisher case. The entire violent crimes unit, all crime scene specialists, and any additional personnel that could be spared were assigned to the investigation.

While the CSI team processed the scene and analyzed evidence, detectives dug into their suspect's background. They discovered this seemingly devoted father and husband was, in fact, a modern-day Jekyll and Hyde, whose dark side apparently got the better of him. At 40 years of age, Robert Fisher was a volatile loner who spent most of his spare time hunting and fishing in the wilderness. He had served in the navy for a time and had allegedly lied to acquaintances about having been a Navy Seal. What's more, he'd been a volunteer firefighter prior to moving to Arizona—a vocation that would have taught him a thing or two about how to rig a house to explode.

Fisher's contradictions, however, were most apparent in his religious practices and social behavior. He was a practicing Born Again Christian who attended church on a regular basis, yet he also frequented seedy strip joints and was known to cheat on his wife.

Fisher's parents had gone through a contentious divorce when he was in his early teens. The divorce was so traumatic, he never really recovered from it. He often told friends he would never subject his own children to the pain and anguish that comes with a failed marriage. Despite his aversion to divorce, there was no denying that the Fishers' marriage was on the rocks. Fisher's violent temper and controlling personality had taken their toll on Mary. Neighbors reported hearing the couple bickering and brawling frequently. And it appeared that Mary had made up her mind to seek a divorce, the one move Fisher could not abide.

Ten days after the investigation into the triple homicide began, Mary's SUV and the family dog were found. They'd been abandoned about 100 miles north of Scottsdale in the Tonto National Forest. A squad of law enforcement officials descended on the area—a mountainous and heavily forested region known for its numerous caves. For the next few days, trackers from the nearby White Mountain Apache Tribal Police along with dozens of others scoured the area in search of the fugitive. Certain Fisher was laying low in one of the many caves in the forest, they searched each one. However, no trace of him was found. Despite all of the investigators' efforts to track him down, Robert Fisher, it seemed, had managed to slip away.

On June 29, 2002, Robert William Fisher, "an alleged triple murderer," was added to the FBI's Ten Most Wanted Fugitives list. "Fisher is being sought for his alleged involvement in the brutal death of his family in Arizona. He should be considered armed and extremely dangerous," the press release stated. Despite several sightings and a $50,000 reward for information leading to his arrest, Robert Fisher remains at large.

CHAPTER 7

The Bloody Footprint

The uniformed officer was waiting outside the two-story brick farmhouse when
Sergeant Mike Illes and Constable Don
Shearer arrived. Illes glanced at his watch, not-
ing it was already 4:30 p.m. There was no way
he would make it home in time for the party his
wife had planned for their son's fifth birthday
that evening. In fact, he'd be lucky if he made
it home that night at all. A five-year veteran of
the Ontario Provincial Police Central Region

Forensic Identification Unit, Illes knew that processing a crime scene such as this could take anywhere from a few days to a few weeks. He had the feeling this one would take several days at least. Because he and his team usually pulled 12 to 18 hour shifts while working on a case, he decided he'd better call home and wish his son a happy birthday before getting to work.

The call reporting a 1045—the code for a suspicious death—had come in about an hour earlier. The body of an elderly male had been discovered at an isolated farmhouse outside of Cambellford, a small town approximately 25 miles east of Peterborough, Ontario. Illes's detachment was located in Peterborough, however, it covered a large territory that extended from the southern tip of Algonquin Park to the north shore of Lake Ontario.

In a unit that dealt with only about a dozen murders each year, it was always interesting to work a homicide case. As lead investigator on the case, Illes was responsible for coordinating the team and making all procedural decisions. While driving to the scene, he ran through the various processes involved and considered the different approaches they might take regarding the investigation. His training and experience had taught him that it was impossible to tell beforehand exactly what search method would be most appropriate. The crime scene itself dictates the approach. All the same, Illes found running through the possibilities in advance helped him to focus.

"It's a mess in there," the officer said as Illes and Shearer grabbed their kits from the van and started toward the house. "Looks like quite a struggle took place. The victim was beaten and stabbed several times ... probably a home invasion gone wrong. No sign of a forced entry, though. Door must have been unlocked, or the old guy let the perp in."

The victim, 76-year-old Frank Johnson*, was

---

* Name has been changed

the owner of the house. Apparently he didn't live there alone. He had taken in a female boarder named Carolyn Jones* a few months earlier. When Illes and Shearer arrived, Jones was being questioned by the detectives working the case. When asked about her whereabouts at the time of the murder, Jones claimed to have been at a friend's house in town.

The lowering skies were threatening rain, so the investigators quickly set to work processing the exterior of the house before valuable evidence was washed away. The house was a plain brick structure with a wooden summer kitchen attached at the back. It had been determined that the killer had entered and exited the scene through the door leading into the kitchen, so Illes and Shearer began their search here. They started by photographing and documenting the exterior. Then the doors and doorframes were dusted for fingerprints and the area searched for trace evidence.

---

* Name has been changed

Just outside the back door, a collection of empty buckets, storm windows, and bits and pieces of lumber surrounded a rusty wringer washer. As Illes picked his way through the debris, he spied a number of fresh-looking cigarette butts in the grass. It was clear someone had recently stood outside the door smoking one cigarette after another. The sergeant snapped a few photographs of the butts before plucking them from the grass and placing them in an evidence envelope. These would be sent to the lab for DNA testing.

The temperature inside the musty, old farmhouse was noticeably cooler than it was outside. As investigators approached the dining room, they caught a whiff of the putrid odor of decomposition and heard the familiar buzzing of bluebottles. The victim had been dead for at least 24 hours, and although the house had been closed up, several bluebottles, drawn by the scent of blood, had managed to squeeze in through gaps around the windows and doors and now hovered around the body.

The victim was lying face up in a pool of blood on the dining room floor. He was wearing nothing but a pair of briefs, and his arms were strapped to his upper torso by what appeared to be an electrical cord torn from a nearby lamp. He had been bludgeoned and stabbed several times. His face was a blackened, bloody mess. The post mortem would reveal that his skull had been fractured and several ribs broken by a heavy, elongated instrument such as a baseball bat. Illes noted the man had stab wounds on his legs and several defensive wounds on his hands. The knife attack had been so savage that one finger was almost completely severed.

Before processing it for trace evidence and then releasing it to the coroner, Illes and Shearer photographed the body. A thorough check for trace would be conducted at the autopsy in Toronto the next day, but because ephemeral evidence could easily be lost during transport, Illes wanted to process the body before it was zipped into a body bag and sent to the morgue.

Once they'd attended to the body and the deputy coroner had removed it, the investigators turned their attention to their surroundings. As Illes surveyed the scene, he noted there was significant impact blood spatter from the beating in the area where the body was found. Evidence of wiping and hair transfer patterns also appeared on the floor in that area. Having recently completed blood spatter pattern analysis training with the RCMP, Illes was particularly intrigued by the spatter and what it revealed about the attack.

As he studied the blood spatter, Illes tried to visualize the sequence of events leading to Johnson's death. From the looks of things, the old man had been using the living room as a bedroom. A bed was set up in the corner, and his work boots, pants, and shirt were scattered around it, indicating he'd undressed there before climbing into bed. A blood-soaked comforter on the floor near the body suggested he'd likely been awakened by the sound of an intruder in the next room. Because he was wearing nothing but his underwear, he'd wrapped the comforter around himself and gone out to confront the perpetrator. The hair transfer patterns and wiping on the floor, along with the defensive wounds on the victim's hands, indicated he had put up a considerable fight before he died.

As Illes scanned the floor around the area where the body was found, he noticed a few bloody footwear impressions on the scuffed hardwood. It appeared the suspect had stepped in the blood and then tracked it across the floor. This was a remarkable stroke of luck for the investigators. Illes placed a measuring scale next to the prints and prepared to photograph them. Once a suspect was apprehended, they'd be able to compare the photos with the soles of the suspect's shoes. If these matched, it would place the killer at the scene. Since there had been paramedics and others through the scene earlier, however, he'd have to check their footwear first in order to eliminate them as the source of the print.

Thinking there might be more bloody prints in the area that weren't visible to the naked eye, Illes mixed up some Leucomalachite Green. As he sprayed the solution around in strategic spots, about a dozen bright green footprints materialized. Interestingly, three distinctly different sets of footwear were apparent. Up to that point, the investigators had assumed there was only one suspect involved in the homicide; now it appeared there may have been at least three. One set of prints was fairly small—too small to be those of a grown man. Illes felt certain they belonged to either a young boy or possibly a woman.

After photographing the impressions, Illes scanned the remainder of the room. On the floor in a corner of the room, a single passive drop of blood caught his attention. As he examined it he realized the circular drop had fallen from above, not flown across the room as impact spatter. Certain this wasn't the victim's blood, but that of the killer, Illes swabbed it for DNA testing.

In the meantime, Shearer methodically inched his way around the cramped dining room. For some reason, several tables surrounded by mismatched chairs had been crammed into the room, as though the owner had intended to throw a bridge party or some similar event. The jumble of furniture made it difficult for the investigators to move around without disturbing anything. As he worked his way across the room, a full-sized chest freezer shoved into a corner caught Shearer's attention. It was odd that a freezer was in the dining room in the first place; odder still was the fact that a padlock had been installed on its lid. When he moved close enough to get a good look, he realized the lock had been sawed off. "Hey, Mike. Come and get a look at this," he shouted. "Why do you suppose someone would put a padlock on a freezer?"

While Illes and Shearer processed the scene, detectives were out canvassing the neighborhood and investigating leads. Johnson's boarder, Carolyn Jones, was a person of particular interest.

The 37-year-old welfare recipient was frequently seen around town with a couple of rough characters. One, 32-year-old Jeff Owens*, occasionally worked as a manual laborer. The other, 39-year-old David Gerard*, was also on social assistance.

When Illes informed the detectives about the padlock on the freezer and the different footprints discovered at the scene, they began to suspect that Johnson's boarder wasn't as innocent as she maintained. Although they were fairly sure the killer was a male, they felt Jones was involved somehow.

During Jones's stay at his place, Johnson had probably ranted to her about his mistrust of banks—about what highway robbers all bankers were, and how you were better off keeping your lifesavings in a sock under your mattress. It wouldn't take a genius to figure out where he kept his stash. The padlock on the freezer was a dead giveaway. Jones likely mentioned the

---

* Names have been changed

stash of cash to Owens and Gerard, and before long, a plan to steal it was in the works. Jones could merely leave the door open one night and signal when it was safe to enter.

On September 15, a full four days after they began processing the scene, Illes and Shearer finally completed their job and headed back to the lab. Although the murder weapon hadn't been recovered, they had collected plenty of other evidence, including the sawed off lock, the bloody shoeprints, the cigarette butts, tire tracks, some fingerprints, and the blood. Now it was time to begin analyzing the evidence.

The cigarette butts and blood swabs were submitted for DNA testing. It would be several months, however, before they would receive the results of these tests. In the meantime, the investigators analyzed the fingerprints. They had scoured the crime scene from top to bottom looking for prints. They'd even gone so far as to spray the walls of the farmhouse with ninhydrin, a highly toxic solvent that reveals latent prints on porous surfaces. All they managed to find, though, were a few prints on the door leading from the living room to the dining room, directly above the spot where the body was discovered. Unfortunately, these turned out to be the victim's.

The tire tracks were also a disappointment. They belonged to the ambulance that responded to the 911 call. However, after eliminating the footwear of everyone who had attended the scene, investigators still hadn't turned up the shoes that matched the bloody prints.

In order to make a case, the team had to find the knife and baseball bat used to kill Frank Johnson, as well as the bloodied shoes. Based on the evidence they had at that point, a warrant was issued to search the residence of Jeff Owens, the main suspect in the case. Investigators received the warrant several days after the murder—ample time for the killer to dispose of any evidence linking him to the crime.

It wasn't long after they began searching

Owens' residence, however, that the knife was found. Incredibly, Owens hadn't even bothered to clean the victim's blood off its shaft. In addition to the knife, the search also turned up the shoes that matched the bloody prints found at the scene. Despite the discovery of half a dozen baseball bats stashed in a closet, the one used to bludgeon Johnson to death wasn't recovered. Even without the murder weapon, investigators had sufficient evidence to charge Owens with the first-degree murder of Frank Johnson.

When confronted with the evidence held by the prosecution, Jeff Owens decided to plead guilty to the lesser charge of second-degree murder rather than take his chances with a trial. He was sentenced to life with no parole. His accomplices, Carolyn Jones and David Gerard, were charged with robbery. Jones was tried and found guilty; however, David Gerard died of a heart attack before his case went to trial.

CHAPTER 8

The Future

Each week, *CSI* fans are beguiled by the astonishing array of state-of-the-art, high-tech forensic equipment at the disposal of the fictional Las Vegas crime lab. What could possibly be cooler than those tiny ALS lights that cause seminal fluids and fingerprints to fluoresce? Then there's the portable super glue fuming equipment, the smart boards, the virtual crime scene sketch software, and high-powered scanning electron microscopes.

Critics of the show slam it for the glitzy gadgetry and stress that much of it is futuristic or highly exaggerated. In fact, much of the technology portrayed on the show is in use in many crime labs today. And what doesn't exist yet isn't far off.

Forensic technology and equipment is constantly evolving. For example, forensic light sources are becoming smaller, more portable, and less expensive all the time. A little over a decade ago, finding fingerprints with light sources involved working with large, prohibitively expensive lasers that were tied to the lab bench. Researchers then discovered fingerprints could be made to fluoresce with a strong blue light. This prompted the invention of ALS lights, which are powerful white lights with colored filters that can be transported to a crime scene and plugged into a wall socket. The latest models—those featured on *CSI*—are hand held, cordless models.

The portable super glue fuming units are

also currently in use by actual crime scene investigators. However, these units are extremely hazardous. super glue fumes are highly toxic; consequently, investigators must wear decidedly unattractive protective gear when using this technique, something the fictional characters of *CSI* don't bother with.

Software and databases are always prominently featured on *CSI*. In fact, one of the most impressive effects on the show is the IAFIS search for matching fingerprints. The computer flips through hundreds of prints in seconds. When it gets a hit, the latent print is automatically transposed over the known print from the database. In addition, the program also points out each of the matching characteristics and declares the print a positive match. In reality, current automated systems, such as IAFIS, don't yet have the capability to do overlays as they appear on *CSI*. But, as fingerprint expert Lee Fraser points out, with the use of Photoshop and other software programs, a thinned image can be made by the investigator and transposed over the known print. No doubt, in the not too distant future, databases will have the capacity to generate overlays automatically.

Fingerprinting has always been accepted as a practical and inexpensive means to iden-tify criminal suspects. Today, however, it's be-ing used to identify more than just the criminal population. Since the terrorist attacks of 9/11, concerns about security have become a top priority in North America and Europe. Officials have become painfully aware of the vulner-ability of government and corporate buildings, airports, and public transit systems. Much has been done to plug the gaps in security in these areas in recent years. For example, many corpo-rations and government agencies now require that all employees be fingerprinted.

Establishing fingerprint registries is a fast, unobtrusive, and relatively inexpensive method to determine and monitor identification. (It currently takes less than two seconds to search

IAFIS for matching prints.) With this in mind, Lee Fraser foresees a day when all airports will be equipped with digital scanning devices. Before boarding a plane, passengers will have their fingerprints scanned and checked as they pass through security.

DNA. DNA. DNA.

The single greatest advancement in the field of forensic science over the past century is, without question, the invention of DNA profiling. Since its inception 20 years ago, DNA fingerprinting has evolved by leaps and bounds. Advances in technology and methodology over the past decade have made DNA testing much more efficient and the results far more compelling.

One of the most important developments in DNA testing in recent years has been the invention of the polymerase chain reaction (PCR) machine. Because it greatly reduces the amount of biological materials required to generate a DNA profile, PCR has been an incredible boon to crime scene investigation. In order to establish a profile in the past, scientists required at least several micrograms of DNA. Today, however, they can establish a profile using mere nanograms of genetic material.

Because of these advances, DNA profiling is currently regarded as the most reliable and effective means to identify suspects and victims. As DNA testing is further refined, however, taking measures to avoid cross contamination will also become more important. Therefore, in the future, collection methods will undoubtedly be honed and transformed. Currently, crime scene investigators are discouraged from smoking, chewing gum, or handling items, such as the telephone, at the scene. "This will become much more critical as DNA [testing] becomes more sensitive," says Ron Singer, past president of the American Academy of Forensic Science and the crime lab director for the Tarrant County Medical Examiner's Office in Fort Worth, Texas. Singer predicts, "It's going to become much more incumbent upon the crime scene investigator to wear gloves. To change those gloves after they have collected certain items, and before they collect other evidence, because you want to avoid contaminating one item with matter from another item. ... I don't know if it's going to change *what's* collected, just *how* it's collected."

Like all technology today, the trend in forensic equipment is toward compactness. "In most cases now, DNA analysis is becoming faster and much more miniaturized," says Singer. He adds, "I would say that within the next five or ten years there will be handheld devices that you would take to the scene. You'll actually be able to load a sample onto this device at the crime scene, and by the time you get it back to the laboratory you'll be able to insert it into some sort of reader and get a DNA profile."

Not only will the equipment and collection methods become more efficient in future, DNA testing will also become more refined and the information it yields will be far more specific than it is today. Currently, scientists can only determine the sex of the donor. Soon, however, they'll be able to ascertain a broad range of characteristics. "We are looking at coding regions, particularly looking for eye color and hair color," notes Singer; "So I don't think it's that far in the future when we will be able to analyze the sample and give you some investigative information along the lines of what [the suspect's] natural hair color is, what the natural eye color is, even skin tone, or the amount of pigmentation in the skin."

Despite the ascendancy of DNA typing, it's unlikely to replace all other methods of identifying suspects entirely. There will always be crime scenes where no DNA is recovered. In such cases, predicts Singer, "You're still going to have to turn to the old standards. You're still going to have to turn to trace analysis—still going to have to rely on the firearms examiner to determine whether or not a bullet was fired from a particular gun, and even to provide you with information about a particular gun. You're still going to have to rely on the anthropologist to at least give you some up-front stuff about the description of the skeletal remains. And then you go to DNA. So these things are not going to go away, but I think they're going to be modified somewhat in their applicability to science overall and to their importance within the grand scheme of things."

A CSI Timeline

1835 London policeman Henry Goddard traces a bullet to the weapon that discharged it by comparing the marks on the bullet to those on the mold from which it was made.

1858 Sir William Hershel, a British official serving in India, conceives of the idea of using fingerprints as a system of identification and begins using fingerprints to identify his employees.

1889 Alexandre Lacassagne proves that the striations on a bullet can be matched to the rifling inside the barrel of the gun that fired it.

1901   Scotland Yard becomes the first police force in the world to adopt the Henry System of fingerprint identification.

1910   Edmond Locard sets up the first forensic lab in France.

1911   Thomas Jennings becomes the first person in the United States to be convicted and sentenced to death based on fingerprint evidence.

1914   In Montreal, Quebec, Wilfred Derome establishes the first forensic laboratory in North America. J. Edgar Hoover reportedly made two visits to Derome's "medico–legal laboratory."

1923   The Bureau of Forensic Ballistics is founded in New York.

1925   Calvin Goddard and Phillip Gravelle invent a microscope to compare spent bullets, known as the comparison microscope.

1929 Calvin Goddard matches bullet casings to the guns used in the St. Valentine's Day Massacre.

1930s Thomas Gonzales introduces the first test for gunshot residue, known as the dermal nitrate test.

1932 The FBI's first forensic lab becomes operational.

1936 The lifecycle of blowfly maggots is used to estimate time of death in the Buck Ruxton investigation.

1937 Luminol is first used as a presumptive test for blood.

1983 Chemist Kary Mullis invents polymerase chain reaction (PCR), the process used to replicate DNA.

1986 DNA fingerprinting, developed by Alec Jeffreys at the University of Leicester in England, is used for the first time to

identify and convict Colin Pitchfork of the murders of two young girls.

1999 IAFIS, the FBI's Integrated Automated Fingerprint Identification System, becomes operational. This database now contains the fingerprints of 65 million individuals.

2000 The prime time drama *CSI: Crime Scene Investigation* begins airing on CBS.

2002 *CSI*'s spin-off, *CSI: Miami,* airs for the first time.

2004 CBS introduces *CSI: New York,* the second spin-off of the popular primetime drama.

Amazing Facts and Figures

- Centuries ago, the Chinese and Babylonians used fingerprints as a kind of signature on documents and contracts. It wasn't until the 19th century, however, that the unique characteristics of individual fingerprints were discovered and recorded.

- One of the largest, most sophisticated crime labs in the world is that of the Federal Bureau of Investigation. The first FBI forensic lab was set up in 1932. In its first year of operation, the lab processed approximately 1,000 pieces of evidence. Today, the bureau's forensic investigations number approximately one million per year.

- According to the Bureau of Justice Statistics, there were 33 federal, 203 state or regional, 65 county, and 50 municipal forensic labs in the United States. in 2002 (the most recent date for which statistics are available). These labs employed roughly 9,400 full-time employees.

HOMICIDE DEFINITIONS

1st degree murder (cold-blooded)
requires proof of premeditation,
deliberation, and malice
(planning, coolness, scheming)

2nd degree murder (hot-blooded)
requires proof of malice
aforethought and intent to do
bodily harm (for all practical
purposes, malice aforethought is
the same as premeditation)

Voluntary manslaughter (heat of
passion) requires proof of
provocation and no time to cool
off (self defense is a common
defense)

Involuntary manslaughter
(accidents) require at least a
reckless disregard of the
consequences (insanity is a
common defense)

CAUSE OF DEATH
(AVERAGE ODDS FOR AMERICANS)

Disease
1 in 1.3

Heart Attack
1 in 3

Cancer
1 in 5

Auto Accident
1 in 42

Suicide
1 in 81

Homicide
1 in 84

- According to the 2002 Census of Publicly Funded Forensic Crime Laboratories in the United States (published in February 2005), the nation's public forensic crime labs ended 2002 with more than 500,000 backlogged requests for forensic services, compared with 290,000 requests that were backlogged at the beginning of the year—a 70 percent increase.

- Publicly funded forensic crime laboratories in the United States received more than 2.7 million new requests during 2002.

- The most frequently requested public forensic laboratory service in the U.S. is the identification of controlled substances, which accounts for about half of all requests. Toxicology samples and latent-print requests were the next most common types of services requested.

- During the investigation of the Oklahoma City bombing in 1995, hundreds of FBI and ATF agents painstakingly sifted through tons of rubble and debris, seeking leads. In the weeks following the blast, approximately 13,000 pieces of evidence were collected and processed. Finally, a scorched and twisted part of a truck axle was pulled from the wreckage. The serial number on the axle was traced to Ryder Rentals in Miami. This led to a Ryder office in Junction City, Kansas, and ultimately to prime suspect Timothy McVeigh.

- As its name implies, the lab of the U.S. Department of Justice's Bureau of Alcohol, Tobacco, Firearms and Explosives (ATF) is primarily dedicated to investigating crimes that involve alcohol, tobacco, firearms, explosives, and fire debris analysis. ATF has over 110 professionals employed in four different labs. In addition, each lab has a mobile unit equipped to process evidence at the scene of an explosion or fire. In 2003, ATF investigated 1,884 incidents involving explosives and arson.

- The first Royal Canadian Mounted Police (RCMP) forensic lab was established in Regina, Saskatchewan, in 1937, in a cramped room in the Officer's Mess. Today, the RCMP boasts six crime labs, which employ approximately 300 forensic scientists.

- The homicide rate has generally been declining in North America since the mid-1970s.

- Canada's homicide rate of 1.73 victims per 100,000 was about one-third of that of the United States (5.69 per 100,000) and was slightly

lower than that of England and Wales (1.93),
but higher than France (1.65) and Australia
(1.63).

• There are around 25,000 homicides a year in
the United States and 548 homicides (in 2003)
in Canada. Homicide is a crime with a relatively
good clearance rate. In the U.S., 65 to 85 percent
of homicides are solved each year.

• The legal signs of death are: no respiration;
no heartbeat; no pulse; fingernails don't flush
when pressed; eyelids don't close when lifted;
pupils don't dilate when exposed to light.

• After death, the body begins to cool down to
the outside or room temperature. At death, the
body begins to drop from its normal temperature of 98.6° F (37° C). It drops 3° F the first hour
and 1° F each subsequent hour. Then, after 30
hours, it begins to warm up again because of
heat generated by decomposition.

What Others Say

"The CSI effect is basically the perception of near-infallibility of forensic science in response to the TV show. This TV show comes on and everyone starts watching it—including the cops and prosecutors—and submissions to forensic laboratories go through the roof."

Max Houck
Forensic Science Professor,
West Virginia University

"We *do* have same-day DNA results, but no one wants to watch a TV show where it takes four months to get results."

Anthony Zuiker
Creator of CSI

"The crime scene is the most dynamic, most important aspect of the total investigation. The integrity and the security of the crime scene are crucial."

Henry C. Lee
Criminalist

"One thing they don't show on TV is the systematic approach we take to the crime scene. We only get one crack at it, so it has to be done right."

Inspector Neil Fraser
RCMP Forensic Identification Services

"By and large, police work — work in a crime lab, things like that — is not as spectacularly exciting as they would have you believe on television. ... We don't interrogate suspects, and we don't drive Hummers. And perhaps, with some exceptions, our staff, myself included, do not look like models."

Ron Singer
Crime lab director and past
president of the American
Academy of Forensic Science

"It is safe to postulate that many of the crimes of past generations could have been solved with impunity if modern forensic tools had been available and used"

Henry C. Lee
Criminalist

"One great thing about *CSI* is that it's made science accessible and interesting to the general public again."

Doug Strongman
Forensic Entomologist

"I don't try to debunk [*CSI*] completely; instead, I try to point out their limitations. We don't have those cool little flashbacks. God, I wish we did!"

Marilyn Miller
Forensic Science Professor
Virginia Commonwealth University

Select Bibliography

Books

Baden, Michael, M.D. and Roach, Marion. *Dead Reckoning: The New Science of Catching Killers.* New York: Simon & Schuster, 2001.

Erzinçlioglu, Zakaria. *Forensics: True Crime Scene Investigations.* New York: Barnes & Noble Books, 2002.

Greenshields, Malcolm R. and Scheurman, Gordon D. *The Crime Scene: Criminalistics, Science, and Common Sense.* Toronto: Prentice Hall, 2001.

Hertzog, Arthur. *The Woodchipper Murder.* New York: Henry Holt, 1989.

Lee, Henry C. with O'Neil, Thomas W. *Cracking Cases: The Science of Solving Crimes.* New York: Prometheus Books, 2002.
Lee, Henry and Labriola, Jerry. *Famous Crimes Revisited: A Forensic Scientist Reexamines the Evidence.* New York: Berkley Books, 2001.

Moose, Charles A. and Flemming, Charles. *Three Weeks in October: The Manhunt for the Serial Sniper.* New York: Dutton, 2003.

Owen, David. *Hidden Evidence: The Story of Forensic Science and How it Helped to Solve 40 of the World's Toughest Crimes.* London: Quintet, 2000.

Platt, Richard. *Crime Scene: The Ultimate Guide to Forensic Science.* London: DK Publishing, 2003.

Ragle, Larry. *Crime Scene.* New York: Avon, 1995.

Web Sites
America's Most Wanted: http://www.amw.com/fugitives/brief.cfm?id=25245

ATF Online: http://www.atf.treas.gov/labs/index.htm

"Detective Edward O. Heinrich and the Mail Train Murders Part 1 and 2" http://www.trivia-library.com/c/detective-edward-o-heinrich-and-the-mail-train-murders-part-1.htm

Fattig, Paul. "The Last Great Train Robbery." http://angelfire.com/wa/andyhiggins/Greattrainrobbery.html

FBI Homepage: http:// www.fbi.gov/homepage.htm

Gado, Mark. "All About the Woodchipper Murder Case." http://www.crimelibrary.com/notorious_murders/family/woodchipper_murder/index.html

Papers and Articles

Benecke, Mark. "A Brief History of Forensic Entomology." *Forensic Science International* 120 (2001) 2–14.; Borger, Julian. "Captured in their sniper's nest: Gulf veteran and the teenager." *The Guardian,* October 25, 2002.; _____. "Dropped clues that led police to sniper." *The Guardian,* October 25, 2002.; Chandler, Anne. "Nabbed!" *Reader's Digest,* February 2005.; Farley, Christopher John. "The Case is Made, for Now." *Time.* July 17, 1995.; Fraser, G.N. "A Murder in Moncton." *Canadian Society of Forensic Science Journal* Vol. 34. No. 4, 2001.; Horwitz, Sari and Ruane, Michael E. "Card's Discovery Opened Line of Communication." *Washington Post,* October 5, 2003.; _____. "Frustrations—and Finally a Breakthrough." *Washington Post,* October 7, 2003.; Kluger, Jeffrey. "How Science Solves Crimes." *Time,* October 21, 2002. Vol.160, Iss. 17.; Lacayo, Richard. "Flesh and Blood." *Time,* July 11, 1994.; Murphy, G.K. "Tragedy at Tunnel 13. The d'Autremont Brothers and 'The Edison of Crime Detection.'" *American Journal of Forensic Medicine and Pathology,* 1987 March 8 (1): 71–4.; Pope, Charles. "In Fear of a Serial Sniper." *Macleans,* October 21, 2002.; Ripley, Amanda. "Inside the Sniper Manhunt." *Time,* October 21, 2002. Vol. 160, Iss.17.; Ruane, Micheal E. and Horwitz, Sari. "Pair Mapped Out Their Travels on a Laptop Computer." *Washington Post,* October 6, 2003.; Streisand, Betsy. "Can He Get a Fair Trial?" *U.S. News & World Report,* October 3, 1994, Vol. 117, Iss. 13.; Van Biema, David. "The Burden of Evidence." *Time,* July 18, 1994.

Acknowledgements

I am deeply indebted to many people for their assistance with the creation of this book, particularly Doug Strongman, who first suggested the subject and provided guidance, information, and encouragement throughout its formation. Many thanks are due also to each of the forensic investigators and experts who generously shared their time, stories, and valuable insights on the subject with me, including Inspector Neil Fraser, Sgt. Mike Illes, Lee Fraser, Sgt. Donald Bellendier, Inspector Paula Dionne, Brian Yamashita, Ron Singer, Vaughn Bryant, Vic Gorman, Gail Anderson, and Veronica Stintson.

Heartfelt thanks to everyone at Altitude Publishing, particularly Kara Turner for her insights, guidance, and suggestions. I'm also grateful to my editor, Brendan Wild, whose careful reading and meticulous approach greatly improved the manuscript.

Direct quotes in the text were obtained from *Three Weeks in October: The Manhunt for the Serial Sniper,* by Charles A. Moose and Charles Flemming, and *Cracking Cases: The Science of Solving Crimes,* by Henry C. Lee with Thomas W. O'Neil.

Photo Credits

Cover: AP Photo; page 8: AP Photo/Dylan Moore; pages 9 & 10: Science Photo Library; page 11: Lee Fraser; page 12: AP Photo; page 13 (top): Sgt. Mike Illes; page 13 (bottom): Neil Fraser.